The Wars of the Roses

Great Wars of the World

History Nerds

Published by History Nerds, 2022.

While every precaution has been taken in the preparation of this book, the publisher assumes no responsibility for errors or omissions, or for damages resulting from the use of the information contained herein.

THE WARS OF THE ROSES

First edition. May 16, 2022.

Copyright © 2022 History Nerds.

ISBN: 979-8215333495

Written by History Nerds.

Also by History Nerds

Celtic History
Ireland

Great Wars of the World
World War 1
World War 2
The Napoleonic Wars: One Shot at Glory
The Serbian Revolution: 1804-1835
Peace Won by the Saber: The Crimean War, 1853-1856
The Wars of the Roses

Irish Heroes
Grace O'Malley: The Pirate Queen of Ireland
William Butler Yeats: Nobel Prize Winning Poet
Scáthach
Finn McCool

The History of the Vikings

Vikings
Longships on Restless Seas

The Rise and Fall of Empires
Rome: The Rise and Fall

Standalone
The History of the United Kingdom
The History of Ireland
The History of America
Stalin
The Fiery Maelstrom of Freedom
The History of Scotland
Robert the Bruce
William Wallace: Scotland's Great Freedom Fighter
The History of Wales

Table of Contents

The Wars of the Roses
1455-1487

Introduction

About empty thrones, a lot can be said. Throughout history, both ancient and near modern, a lack of an heir and the sudden death of a beloved monarch always meant trouble. When the position of a king is up for grabs, a lot of eager hands come forward. Pretenders and would-be heirs, cousins and nephews, bastard sons and daughters - they all come forward staking their claim to the throne. In the history of Medieval England, such episodes were many. Usurpers who oust kings and heirs, pretenders with long forgotten dynastic claims: many once fought for the lucrative throne of the English Kingdom. However, by far the most important of all these historic episodes lasted from 1455 to 1487 - 32 long years of struggle and bloodshed in England. And that episode was known as the *Wars of the Roses.* These wars ravaged England, pitting two competing cadet families of the royal House of Plantagenet - York and Lancaster. Their supporters, the Lancastrians and Yorkists, descended into bitter warfare over the throne. For their symbols they took red and white roses, respectively - thus giving the name to the conflict.

The Wars of the Roses were a complex, long-lasting affair, pitting many rivaling nobles against one another and greatly ravaging England in the process. The nation was ravaged through and through, the nobility decimated in the process, and the fate of the English Kingdom was forged anew. It was a bloody gateway to a new age in England, a crossing point from the aging Medieval Period to the modern notions of the Renaissance. In many ways, it was a war that had to be fought, so the fate of England could be decided. The Wars of the Roses inspired many authors over the centuries, most notably the famed Shakespeare and his plays, and in the more modern times George R. R. Martin, who's iconic *"Game of Thrones"* books are heavily akin to these historic

English wars. Feuding noble houses, powerful lords and pretenders to the throne, bastard sons and bloody battles - the Wars of the Roses have it all!

Chapter I

The history of England between 1370 and 1480 was marked by a string of bloody wars and much destruction. However, at the same time, it was a period of consolidation of England, as well as of its (at the time) traditional enemy across the channel - France. The two nations have been embroiled in a bloody conflict over the French throne, known popularly as the Hundred Years' War. This clash lasted from May 1337, until October 1453. The war arose from the questions of inheritance of the French throne: the French King Phillip VI laid claim to it, as did the English King, Edward III. The conflict ended as a general defeat for England, which lost all its pretensions and continental possessions in France, except for Calais. During this era of warfare, England descended into a difficult era. It was a time of lawlessness, of bloodshed and wanton death. The countryside was rife with brigands and outlaws, deserters and cutthroats that gave no peace to the common folk. And the troubles that arose amongst the dynastic pretenders to the throne did not help the matter, not one bit.

As we said, the Wars of the Roses refer to the struggle of the two cadet branches of one royal house - the Plantagenets. Oddly enough, throughout the English history, the reigns of the Plantagenet Kings were always beset with trouble of some sort - both internal and external. And many of these troubles arose over the question of the contests for the throne. As a matter of fact, one should not be surprised to know that many pretenders to the royal throne did not hesitate to openly usurp that position if they considered the king weak in any way. Younger brothers and ambitious cousins often stirred trouble and pushed the nation towards a civil war, wanting to seize the power for themselves. The first of the Plantagenet Kings was Henry II Curtmantle, reigning from 1154 to 1189. He was a grandson of Henry I, and a great-grandson of the famed William the Conqueror. His is the earliest and most iconic example of the troubles that followed this royal dynasty, as Henry II had to fight his way to power. His successors, too, seldom ascended to the throne without considerable trouble following them. Richard I, known as the "Lionheart", ascended to rule with revolt at his heels, and fought many battles throughout his reign. John Lackland, however, his successor, lost the Duchy of Normandy and most of his possessions in France, and had to face a substantial revolt of the barons. However, with each subsequent Plantagenet ruler, the situation continued along its moderately stable trajectory. But in many ways, it was this instability and the questionable success of the Plantagenet rulers that transformed England in a better way. This came from the inability of the Plantagenets to fully exert their control over the barons and the nobility. They were forced to make concessions and compromises, to negotiate and create new laws and agreements, the most famous of those being the "Magna Carta". This document in many ways constrained their royal power but guaranteed financial and military support from the nobles. Thus, the Plantagenets were not seen as absolute monarchs of England but had many duties towards their kingdom and its denizens. By the time of Edward I, - known as the Hammer of the Scots - who reigned from 1272 to 1307, England's conflict with France slowly came to the foreground. Edward II on the other hand, had a disastrous and unorthodox reign, which had to be painstakingly restored back to order by his successor, Edward III. However, during the latter's reign, the Hundred Years' War with France began, ushering England - and Europe - into a wholly new era. But the ultimate defeat in this multi-generation war would leave England troubled with many internal unrests - social, economic, and political. And this unrest was the perfect breeding ground for a period of chaos and civil war. And that period would become known as the Wars of the Roses.

The main issue at hand, when it comes to the Wars of the Roses, is the complex family tree and genealogy of the Plantagenet royal dynasty and its cadet branches. Because, for the most part, it was a complex and widespread family tree, with many nobles who had claims to the English throne. And with these claims, unrest and usurpations were commonplace. Edward III of Windsor was a largely successful Plantagenet King. His reign of 50 years was uncommonly long for that time, and marked with numerous military successes, and the transformation of England into one of the most powerful nations in Europe. But most important is the fact that Edward III had five sons that reached adulthood: and that meant at least five possible heirs to the throne. His sons were Edward the Black Prince, John of Gaunt, Edmund of Langley, Lionel of Antwerp, and Thomas of Woodstock. For these sons, Edward created duchies: John of Gaunt became Duke of Lancaster, Lionel of Antwerp became Duke of Clarence, Thomas the Duke of Gloucester, and Edmund the Duke of York. The Black Prince was also raised to that rank, becoming the 1st Duke of Cornwall. Why is this important? A duchy was somewhat of a novelty in England at that time: Dukedoms were never before conferred to subjects until that point. The creation of several duchies within England meant that these families and their heirs became a wholly new class of nobility, with substantial claims to the English throne and plenty of power to enter into a struggle for it as well. Furthermore, from these sons of Edward III, the two main cadet rival branches of the Plantagenets emerged: the Lancastrians and Yorkists, or Lancaster and York. These rival houses were descendants of two of Edward III's sons: John of Gaunt, Duke of Lancaster - whose son, grandson, and great grandson were Henry IV, Henry V, and Henry VI respectively; and Edmund, Duke of York, whose remote descendants would come to rule as Kings Edward IV and Richard III.

This "new class of nobility" would, in time, begin to show some of the critical mistakes that were inherent to the so-called "bastard feudalism". This term is a modern coinage and a source of much debate, but it nevertheless describes the defects of the ruling society of the time. According to the historians Charles Plummer and William

Stubbs, who were amongst the first to define this term, bastard feudalism is the distinct form of feudal rule that developed in Late Medieval England. The defining feature of bastard feudalism is the fact that the mid-ranking nobles and knights would offer their military, political, and legal support and service to a lord in exchange for power, influence, positions, or money. This in turn, prompted such nobles to be more loyal to their lord, rather than to their king. And in the long run, this caused the power of the crown to weaken further. And in the troublesome times of the Plantagenet rulers after the Hundred Years' War, such a thing was quite unwelcome. Also crucial for this idea of "bastard feudalism" is the unique form of conscription-based levies that appeared during the reign of King Edward I. Historian William Stubbs tells us that *"the feudal levy was replaced with royal payment in return for military service by the great magnates who willingly served the king. Thus, instead of vassals rendering military service when required by the lord, they paid a portion of their income into the lord's treasury. In turn the lord would supplement the owed military service with hired retainers, a sort of private army in full-time service to the lord."*

This meant that lords and magnates now rose in power, owning - in simplest terms - their own private armies: armies that owed allegiance only to their lord. Such an "army" was known as an "affinity", and affinities became the defining part of the so-called "bastard feudalism". The Plantagenet King Richard II struggled during his reign to curb the power of the magnates, and to increase the size of his own affinities in order to stay on top as a monarch. But even so, the system of affinities greatly changed the socio-political situation in England, and the power of the monarch would never be the same again. In many ways, every part of the social caste in England was heavily reliant on one another, but most importantly - reliant for loyalty and service. For example, the leading nobles were - of course - owing their allegiance to the King; the gentry relied on the support of the nobles (magnates), and the "stepped pyramid of allegiances" continued like that. But such a social system was unstable, as it was much akin to dominoes. If instability occurred on any level of the social pyramid, it would have a ripple effect and directly affect all other levels.

When Edward III died in 1377, the question of succession came to the forefront - and troubled many. And - for many historians - it was this unresolved matter of succession that was the underlying cause of the later Wars of the Roses. It has to be noted that, under the rules of *primogeniture*, Edward's heir was secured. However, near the end of his reign, that line of succession "narrowed", as two of his sons, Edward the Black Prince, and Lionel Duke of Clarence, both died before their father, in 1376 and 1368 respectively. This left three surviving sons that had claims to the throne. These were John of Gaunt, Duke of Lancaster, Edmund of Langley, and Thomas of Woodstock. And the rule of primogeniture only made matters worse: the late Black Prince (eldest son of Edward III) had a son of his own, Richard, whose claim to the throne was stronger than that of his uncles, seeing that he was the son of the eldest son. But Richard was a minor, with three adult uncles all pressing their claim. Thus, England stood mutely and watched as the situation unfolded, with inheritance of the throne an uncertainty.

But in the end, the law of primogeniture was followed, and it was after all that young Richard, being just 10 years old at the time, inherited the throne of his grandfather and was crowned as Richard II. However, there was now the question of his own heirs: if Richard II was to die without a legitimate heir, he would have to be succeeded by the descendants of Lionel of Antwerp, the second eldest son of Edward III. However, Lionel's only child was a daughter, Philippa, who was married off into the influential Mortimer family, and had a son - Roger Mortimer. That gave him the best legal claim to the throne after Richard II. However, to make matters much more complex, Edward III issued a legal decree in 1376, which limited the right of succession only to the male line of his heirs. This decree thus placed the descendants of his third son, John of Gaunt, ahead of the descendants of Lionel of Clarence. In historiographic terms, the situation was a proper conundrum. And that conundrum wasn't at all helped by the fact that all of the possible claimants to the throne were eager to press their cause and get what they wanted above all - power and wealth.

The reign of the boy-king, Richard II, was rather unstable and controversial for the time, especially when considering the fact that he reigned without a regency, as was befitting his youth. This was done as to deprive his uncle, John of Gaunt, from the chance to assume the regent role and thus wield considerable legitimate power within the realm. This fact, and Richard's youth, caused a further gap between the monarch and his nobles, further deteriorating the situation. Oddly enough, young Richard II was a moderately competent ruler, judging by the moderate length of his reign. One of the first crises with which he had to deal early on was the so-called Peasants Revolt in 1381, or the Wat Tyler Rebellion. The revolt was the result of growingly unpopular poll taxes that exerted pressure on the poor peasant class. The poll tax demanded a fixed amount of money, to be paid by every liable person, without regard to their material or social status. At the time of the revolt, Richard was just 14 years old, but he dealt with it, nonetheless. The rebels of Wat Tyler entered London, pillaging and issuing demands. Richard II agreed to meet Wat Tyler and declared that the rebels *"should have all that he could fairly grant"*. During the meeting however, Wat Tyler acted *"in a very rude and disgusting fashion before the King's face"*. The situation then escalated, and Wat Tyler was subsequently killed during the meeting. Richard II promptly ended the revolt by hunting down and executing many of the prominent leaders.

Another crisis was of a more political nature and was a serious threat to Richard's royal position. It resulted from the Parliament's conflict with the court favorite and king's close advisor, Lord Chancellor Michael de la Pole. In 1386, the Chancellor requested preposterous tax rates in order to help fund the defense of the realm, since the French invasion was now a looming threat. The Parliament refused outright, instead requesting the immediate removal of the chancellor. This grew in considerable political tension at court, as the boy King Richard II refused to let his favorite go. The nobles of the parliament then threatened the king with deposition, and only then was Richard forced to dismiss Michael de la Pole. Furthermore, the parliament set up a special commission that would help review and control the fragile royal finances for a year. The tensions between him and the chief representatives of the parliament - Thomas of Woodstock, 1st Duke of Gloucester, Richard Fitzalan, 4th Earl of Arundel, and Thomas de Beauchamp, 12th Earl of Warwick - grew immensely, escalating into an armed confrontation between the King's Chief counselor Robert de Vere. The latter was defeated, and that totally crushed the circle of Richard's close supporters. The young King was now compelled to comply with his rivals, who became known as Lords Appellant: the three parliament members we mentioned above were joined with the son of John Gaunt, Henry Bolingbroke, as well as by Thomas de Mowbray, 1st Earl of Nottingham.

Later during his reign, Richard II pursued peace with the French King Charles VI, despite the disapproval of the Parliament, and negotiated a de facto peace agreement on his own, agreeing to marry the French King's daughter, Isabella of Valois, at the time a six-year-old girl. Furthermore, he used the interim period to gain his vengeance upon the Lords Appellant who wronged him several years prior. When John of Gaunt died in 1399, he exiled his son Henry Bolingbroke, declaring his lands and titles forfeit. However, things soon took a turn for the worse: when Richard II left England in May 1399, journeying on a campaign to Ireland, Henry Bolingbroke used the opportunity to return to England and raised the support amongst the dissatisfied nobles. By October 1399, Richard II was formally deposed, and forced to abdicate in favor of Henry Bolingbroke, now King Henry IV. Henry had the full support of the English nobility, amongst whom Richard was highly unpopular, and was also the first ruler of the Lancastrian branch of the Plantagenets.

Chapter II

And so, we are introduced to the House of Lancaster and their background. The major player in the Wars of the Roses, the Lancastrian branch descends from John of Gaunt the Duke of Lancaster, Edward III third surviving son. Henry Bolingbroke, now Henry IV, exercised this descent to claim the throne of England for himself, although he was not the first in line to do so. Edmund Mortimer, a prominent noble and the great-grandson of Edward III had the better claim - but it was not regarded since Edward III gave explicit orders to emphasize only the male line of descent.

The House of Lancaster itself had a sub-branch: the House of Beaufort. This noble house was also descended from John of Gaunt, albeit by his mistress, Katherine Swynford. Such provenance made the house illegitimate, but John of Gaunt secured its survival by legitimating it through an Act of Parliament during his lifetime. Henry IV subsequently removed the house from the line of succession, thus limiting the threats to his own position.

But what about the second player in the Wars of the Roses that we mentioned? What about the House of York? This noble cadet branch of the Plantagenets traced its descent from Edmund of Langley, the *fourth* surviving son of Edward III and the younger brother of John of Gaunt. Their name comes from Langley's title of Duke of York. However, their claim to the throne was not as direct as that of the Lancastrian branch. In fact, it was not direct at all, but rather complex and delicate. For the most part, the Yorkist branch traced its right to the throne to Lionel of Antwerp, the Duke of Clarence, son of Edward III. The second son of Edmund of Langley was Richard of Conisburgh. He had married one Anne de Mortimer, the daughter of the noble Roger Mortimer. And the grandmother of Anne de Mortimer was none other than Philippa of Clarence, the only daughter of Lionel of Antwerp. Thus, the Yorkist branch also had a claim to the throne.

But didn't we say it was very complex and far-reaching? Nevertheless, these opposing claims laid down the foundations of the Wars of the Roses, with power-thirsty noble families and cadet branches vying for the lucrative position of the English King. So, as we can see, the stage was set for a tight and competitive race for the throne. Naturally, Henry IV's ascension to the throne was not met with all-out approval. In fact, an attempt at deposing him occurred almost at once after he became King, by persons still loyal to young Richard II. These were Baron Despenser, Duke of Exeter, Duke of Surrey, and Earl of Salisbury, who in 1400 created a plot to reinstate Richard II to the throne after freeing him from his imprisonment. Alas, their conspiracy was a failure, and all of these nobles were summarily executed for their attempt. At first, Henry IV promised he would not harm young Richard II after the latter abdicated. But after this failed plot, it became clear to him that leaving him alive would be a mistake, as there were still supporters that would pose a threat. Due to this, Richard II died on February 14th, 1400, under unexplained circumstances. At the time he was imprisoned in Pontefract Castle, and it is thought that he was starved to death at the orders of Henry IV. It was a sad end for the ex-King of England. Some theories quickly arose, claiming that Richard was not killed, but was still alive in exile. These were promptly dismissed. Some even claimed that he died a beggar in 1419 and was buried in Stirling.

Still, with the death of Richard II, Henry IV did not receive the peace and approval that he desired. In fact, his predecessor's death only stirred further distress - in Wales. There was great support for Richard II in Wales, whose nobles were by that point very powerful and closely connected to the English royal family. The fact that the ruler they supported was now inexplicably dead nerd deposed, and that numerous other economic and social problems were ravaging the nation, did not sit well with the Welsh. To that end, a general revolt broke out in Wales, led by a prominent Welsh nobleman - *Owain Glyndŵr*. His rebellion was a major stain upon the reign of Henry IV, and lasted until 1415, even after Henry IV no longer ruled. Amongst the many supporters of *Glyndŵr* were the prominent Welsh noble family - the Tudurs of Penmynydd (Anglicized to Tudors). The Tudors were an old aristocratic family from the North of Wales, from Anglesey, and would come to play the defining role in the Wars of the Roses which were by now slowly coming into shape.

This Welsh rebellion was not the only trouble that Henry IV had to deal with during his relatively short reign. He also faced rebellions "at his own court", which were raised by the disaffected House of Percy. The revolt was led by Thomas Percy, 1st Earl of Worcester and Henry Percy, 1st Earl of Northumberland, both of whom were eventually defeated by Henry and executed: the first in 1403 after his defeat at Shrewsbury, and the other in 1408, after his failure at Bramham Moor. Alas, Henry IV did not live to see the Welsh rebellion quelled, as he died in 1413 after reigning some 14 years. In his place came his son and heir, Henry V, known as Henry of Monmouth. Many historians agree that of all the Plantagenet Kings that were ever seated upon the throne of England, Henry V was the most successful. Also known as Henry of Monmouth, he was the King of England from 1413, until his untimely death in 1422. A noted military commander, he was responsible for a string of military successes against France in the Hundred Years' War, which once again established England as the leading power in Europe.

Much like his father, Henry V was faced with a great challenge early in his rule. This challenge was the Southampton Plot, led by Sir Thomas Grey, Baron Scrope, and Richard of Conisburgh. The last one of these was, as we mentioned, the second son of Edmund of Langley, Duke of York, another one of Edward III's many heirs. However, Henry V learned of this plot and quickly had its leaders imprisoned and executed. Thus, he removed any threat to his reign. But even so, he needed a good way to cement his position as a competent King - both at home and abroad. To do this, he decided to rekindle the conflict with France, using his dynastic claim to the French throne, and the reason that the French supported the Welsh revolt, as a pretense to invade France in 1415. Thus began the final phase of the Hundred Years' War, also known as the Lancastrian War.

Almost from the get-go, Henry V began achieving considerable successes. On 22nd September, he managed to capture Harfleur after a siege. His armies, however, were decimated by hunger, illness, and exhaustion. On 25th October, they were surprised by a numerically superior French army that cut off their line of retreat. Against all odds, Henry V stood his ground and won a decisive victory at the legendary Battle of Agincourt, where the English and Welsh longbowmen decimated the French heavy knights and cavalry. The French suffered mind-boggling losses, with 90 to 120 lords and noblemen dying. Agincourt decimated the French nobility, severely shaking the country on the whole. Furthermore, one of the dead noblemen on the English side was none other than the 2nd Duke of York, whose younger brother was Richard of Conisburgh - the failed usurper of Henry's rule.

Thanks to his incredible victory at Agincourt, where he bravely fought in hand-to-hand combat at the frontlines (in comparison to the French King who was clinically insane and not even present), and his subsequent campaigns, Henry V solidified his rule and confirmed the legitimacy of the Lancastrian claim to the throne and their monarchy. By 1420, his campaigns in France proved a success, and the Treaty of Troyes was signed with the French King Charles the Mad. It was a devastating treaty for the French: Henry got to marry the French King's daughter, Catherine of Valois, the French heir to the throne was disinherited, and the future sons of Henry and Catherine were acknowledged as the legitimate heirs to the throne of France. Their first son came to this world on December 6th, 1421 and was also named Henry. He would be the future King Henry VI.

Nevertheless, even with all of his successes - both at home and abroad - the sudden demise of Henry V did not leave England in a solid position. This was due to his unexpected death: Henry V died when he was just 35, after contracting dysentery in one of his campaigns in France. And, as was already the practice, when a monarch dies young, the question of an heir comes to the forefront. Henry VI was barely 9 months old when his father perished. This left England to face a troubling period of regency, until the young king came of age to rule. But England needed a capable leader above all - a leader in the vein of Henry V, who was now no longer at the helm. The king's infancy was always a fertile time for the birth of internal conflicts and feuds, and the absence of an effective monarch inevitably reduced the king's control over the already powerful aristocracy, many of whose members were involved in the contest for political power.

In France, the eldest of Henry V's surviving brothers, John, 1st Duke of Bedford, continued a slow wave of English conquests. This rolled on until 1429, when France suddenly reeled and struck back, especially after the appearance of Joan of Arc, who subsequently stopped the English at Orleans. In 1435, the English suffered further downfalls, especially after John of Bedford died, and the main English ally, the Duke of Burgundy, revolted. With all this at play, the English turned to the defensive role, as it was becoming increasingly apparent that the conquest of France was no longer a realistic possibility. From that point on, the English internal politics were preoccupied with a singular question: whether to continue the war, or to pursue peace with France. The main figures in English politics were Henry Beaufort, the Bishop of Winchester, the uncle of the King, and the popular Humphrey of Lancaster, Duke of Gloucester. In England itself, the high level of riots, for which most of the responsibility was borne by powerful violators against whom it was difficult to obtain legal compensation, was maintained without interruption, and quarrels and conflicts between the nobility eager for new possessions increased in number and violence. But none of these problems were insurmountable when Henry VI, in November 1437, unusually early, at the age of only sixteen, proclaimed the end of his infancy and issued a proclamation to take power.

Still, before this point, the success of the government was laid upon the shoulders of an aristocratic union that ruled England from 1422 and showed a high degree of political responsibility. Thanks to the help of the prominent nobleman, John Lancaster, Duke of Bedford, who successfully lowered the tensions between the bitter rivals - Beaufort and Gloucester - major escalations in internal affairs were avoided. And above all, thanks to the realistic and careful diplomacy, the English could still count on a favorable peace treaty with the French and to keep most of the conquests that Henry V made in France. After all, it was exactly this way of rule that could strive to return some of the financial credibility that England once had, especially once the peace treaty lowered the enormous military expenses that were needed to fuel the war. Henry V was the ideal example to show that a capable and strong monarch could keep the nation afloat and to quell the many arguments between the nobles and the magnates. Due to this, the burdens that his successor, young Henry VI, had to deal with - were immense.

At this time, the claim to the throne of Richard of York was becoming more and more attractive to the magnates of England. Richard of York was the great-grandson of King Edward III, and son of Richard of Conisburgh, who was executed for plotting against Henry V. Now that the suddenly dead king left only a baby boy, and his young brothers had no surviving heirs, the Beaufort family was the only alternative Lancastrian successor to the throne. And that gave the Yorkist house a good chance to seize the throne for themselves. This would become especially attractive to others as the future reign of Henry VI would deteriorate.

Chapter III

For many, Henry V was seen as a highly influential and successful ruler. However, the reign of his successor, Henry VI, is seen by most historians as weak, filled with failures, and all out terrible. Of course, the overall success or unsuccess of his reign has been highly debated over the years by many authors and historians and continues to be discussed even today. Nevertheless, his reign had many shortcomings, most of which contributed to the development of the Wars of the Roses. In many ways, he was a stark contrast to his father: he was seen as timid and shy, opposed to warfare, passive, filled with good intentions, and - according to some - melancholic and mentally unstable. All of these personality traits do not fit well with a monarch of that time, especially considering the fact that England was fighting a losing war in France. Some of Henry VI's policies had a highly detrimental effect on the English society at the time, as well as the nation's politics. His frequent interventions in foreign policy prior to 1450 were seen as disastrous, as was his largely uncontrollable distribution of prominent positions, titles, lands, and offices - mostly to his friends. Many "jumped on the train" in order to benefit from the "generous" character of King Henry VI, for example the Duke of Suffolk, or Lord Saye. In time, a particular "court party" was formed from these friends who plucked all the boons and titles, and they even restricted access to the King at times. Many of the king's contemporaries saw his excessive generosity as very unwise and detrimental.

One of the main issues with Henry's general incompetence was the lack of competent advisors and regents during his early childhood. After all, he was just 9 months old when his father died, and someone had to rule instead of him. However, those who surrounded him were described as "quarrelsome and greedy". His uncle from his father's side, Humphrey, the Duke of Gloucester, pursued his own goals during this time, wanting to be named Lord Protector, and seeking support amongst the people. He was opposed in turn by Henry Beaufort. The two bickered near constantly, and even recalled John, Duke of Bedford, from France in order to mediate between the two of them. The Duke of Bedford, in turn, fought hard to preserve the achievements of Henry V in France, but to no avail. The French were now rallying and reeling back, led by the enigmatic Joan of Arc. Subsequently, the English suffered two devastating defeats, at Orleans and Patay, and most of the achievements by Henry V were completely reversed and made redundant. Eventually, Charles VII ascended to the French throne in 1429. In response to this, the English quickly proceeded with the formal coronation of Henry VI, who became King at age 7, in 1429.

An important event occurs during this time, and it is one that we cannot overlook - for it is essential to the story of the Wars of the Roses. That event is the new marriage of Henry VI's mother, Catherine of Valois. When Henry V died in France and left her widowed, rumors quickly arose that she was having an affair with one Edmund Beaufort, Duke of Somerset. Catherine responded harshly to these allegations and claimed that *"[She] shall marry a man so basely, yet gently born, that my lord regents may not object."* That man turned out to be Owen Tudor (Welsh: *Owain ap Maredudd ap Tudur*), a prominent Welsh nobleman from the influential family of Tudors of Penmynydd. The two married roughly in 1428, and their union quickly produced two surviving sons, Edmund and Jasper Tudor. The two would come to play defining roles in the Wars of the Roses.

In 1437, at age 16, Henry VI came of age to rule. At once, it had become apparent that he had special inclinations to certain members of his retinue and court, especially those who advocated peace in France.

William de la Pole, the 4th Earl of Suffolk, arose in the court as the dominant figure and the King's favorite - he was one of the foremost to seek a diplomatic solution for the conflict in France, rather than continuing the war effort. And as Henry VI would prove to be a meek person, opposed to bloodshed and warfare, William de la Pole quickly resonated with him fully. However, the increasingly popular (amongst the people) Richard of York, and the Duke of Gloucester, too, opposed William de la Pole, as they both favored the continuation of the war in France. The enmity between these parties further escalated when King Henry VI showered the Beauforts and de la Pole with many gifts, grants of land, and important offices - as was common with his generous personality. These gifts further indebted the government and drew away important funds from the war effort in France.

The Earl of Suffolk nevertheless continued his rise to prominence at court, and orchestrated the Treaty of Tours in 1444, which brokered peace between France and England. He also negotiated with success the marriage between Henry and Margaret of Anjou, and thus acquired the strategically important lands of Maine and Anjou in France. This all earned him many promotions from the generous King Henry VI: from Earl he rose to Marquess, and by 1448 to Duke. But throughout all this, he earned substantial animosity from the competing magnates and nobles. In 1447 he accused the Duke of Gloucester of treason, and the latter was arrested. While awaiting trial, the man died, with many suspecting that Suffolk straight out poisoned him. Furthermore, he managed to "get rid" of the influential Richard of York by stripping him of his command in France and instead sending him to govern the distant Lordship of Ireland - for ten years. And thus, William de la Pole became the foremost power at the court, behind the young King. Still, as the English continued to lose lands in France, the finger of blame landed on de la Pole. He attracted many enemies, and they were quick to lay all the blame on him. By 1450, the man was arrested and imprisoned in the Tower of London. Henry VI intervened on his behalf and instead had him exiled for five years. However, enroute to France, William de la Pole was captured and executed by his enemies.

In Suffolk's place came Edmund Beaufort, Duke of Somerset. Being appointed firstly as the new commander of the armies in France (after Richard of York was moved to Ireland), Duke of Somerset did not enjoy a favorable position at court, because he was criticized for the bad state of affairs in France. However, Edmund Beaufort was a close ally of none other than Margaret of Anjou, the wife of Henry VI. The queen virtually held all the control over King Henry, who was seen as meek and pliable. Many suspected that Beaufort was having an affair with the Queen, a matter that was never fully resolved. When King Henry VI had a son in 1453, young boy Edward, many claimed that the child was in fact the son of Edmund Beaufort.

As for Henry VI's controversial foreign policies, the main finger of blame lay on his rapid loss of all the achievements his successful father made in France. Historians today debate whether these losses were entirely the fault of King Henry VI, or of his ill-advising court party. Either way, it is known that Henry VI was generally opposed to warfare and timid, and thus pursued peace with France, particularly after 1445. He secretly offered to surrender the regions of Anjou and Maine to the King of France, which went completely against the policies of the English leading noblemen and the general public, both of whom were highly invested in the English cause in France and in the preceding conquests by Henry V. Because of this, the decision of Henry VI to pursue peace was disastrous and met with an uproar by the nobility.

Economically, England was in an increasingly worsening position. Running such a lengthy war was debilitating for the realm's coffers, and kings often had to raise additional funds to keep the gears of the war machine lubricated. To that end, credits were often raised - in essence loans. These credits were taken from Italian bankers, and in the end created a substantial debt for England. By 1450, the English government was considered *bankrupt*. Its outside debt rose to a staggering £372,000, while its income amounted to just £33,000 annually. A major trade depression emerged at this time, and England was both unable to pay for virtually anything - let alone its credit - and was also unable to make further loans. A great part of this debt was caused by the considerable generosity of King Henry VI, and his "gifts" to friends and supporters, most of them from the Lancastrian side.

By 1459, Henry VI was no longer an active governor of his realms, but rather became a pawn, a presence on the throne of England that was controlled by his closest counselors and his wife Margaret of Anjou. To make matters worse, Henry's mental state was becoming increasingly worse. In 1453, likely after hearing news of English defeat at the Battle of Castillon (seen as the end of the Hundred Years' War), Henry VI suffered a debilitating nervous breakdown, becoming unresponsive to his surroundings for well over a year. Many historians state that Henry's series of mental breakdowns, and his bout of insanity, were inherited from the French King Charles VI "the Mad", to whom Henry was related on his maternal side. This French King suffered from catastrophic bouts of insanity, and at one point attacked his retainers for no reason whatsoever. Either way, Henry VI was in no state to govern the realm, and was thus easily manipulated by his counselors at court. In that very same year, however, his son Edward was born. Henry made no response to the news. Contemporary accounts tell us of the dire state of the King:

"As touching tidings, may it please you to know that at the Prince's coming to Windsor, the Duke of Buckingham took him in his arms and presented him to the King in goodly fashion, beseeching the King to bless him; but the King gave no answer. Nevertheless, the Duke still stayed with the Prince by the King; and when he could have no kind of answer, the Queen came in and took the Prince in her arms and presented him in like form as the Duke had done, desiring that the King should bless him; but all their labor was in vain, for they departed thence without any answer of look from the King, saving only that once he looked on the Prince and cast his eyes down, without any more sign of recognition."

On April 15th, 1450, the English suffered one of the most devastating defeats in the Hundred Years' War. This was the Battle of Formigny, where the English forces were literally massacred by the devastating charge of the French Breton cavalry. This defeat, one of the culminating engagements of the war, allowed the French to reconquer the region of Normandy. In that same year, England had to face internal problems as well. This was the rebellion that arose in Kent, led by one Jack Cade. This violent uprising by the people was seen by many historians as the precursor to the Wars of the Roses. The rebels issued their own manifesto, called the *"Complaint of the Poor Commons of Kent"*, which went into great detail about the issues they had with the crown. They accused the court of extortion, fraud, injustice, and ill-advising of the King. Some of their proclamations are as follows:

"We, consyderyng that the kynge owre sovereyn lorde, by the insaciable covetows malicious pompes, and fals and of nowght browght up certeyn persones, and dayly and nyghtly is abowt his hynesse, and dayly enforme hym that good is evyll and evyll is good..

(We, considering that the king our sovereign lord, by the insatiable covetous malicious pomps, and falls and of nought brought up certain persons, and daily and nightly is about his highness, and daily inform him that good is evil and evil is good.)"

The rebellion of Jack Cade had surprising, but short-lived success. The peasant "army" occupied parts of London and went on to capture and execute James Fiennes, the Lord High Treasurer who was highly unpopular amongst the folk. The treasurer was given a mock trial, declared a traitor, and then beheaded by an angry mob. His head was crudely paraded through London. The rebels began to loot and pillage London, to which the citizens responded with violence. Bloodshed ensued and culminated in a vicious "citizen" battle at the London Bridge. In an attempt to stop the violence, the government (King), offered to pardon all the rebels and sent them home. However, Jack Cade and other prominent leaders of the revolt were later caught and executed. This was a major "insurgency" during Henry VI's rule and a direct reflection of the poor state in which England was at the time. From the 1430s to the 1480s, the period known as the Great Slump raged in England. This economic depression crippled English trade and influenced exports as well. Another crisis was the Great Bullion Famine, a shortage of precious metals that swept through Europe in the 15th century.

However, the rebellion of Jack Cade gave the rising Richard of York a basis to oppose the Royal Government. The man became the focal point of the opposition to the government and the renewed Yorkist claims to the throne. He saw the period of unrest as his chance, and promptly returned from his post in Ireland. However, he was quickly imprisoned during 1452 and 1453, and thus seemingly lost the short power struggle. Meanwhile, Henry VI became increasingly mentally unstable and distanced from all and any affairs of state. This led to a series of catastrophic defeats of his armies in France, which by now were lacking a competent monarch and leader, and funds. First of these critical defeats was in 1450 at Formigny, and then at Castillon in 1453. The latter battle is seen as the culminating engagement that marked the end of the Hundred Years' War. As a result, the English lost all their territorial possessions in France, except Calais. As a direct result of this defeat, the balance of powers in Europe shifted considerably. It is said that Henry VI suffered a complete mental breakdown when hearing of the defeat, and at this point entered his lethargic, distanced mood.

By that point, the atmosphere in England was ripe for a civil war. The lack of central authority meant that the political and economic situation in the nation was becoming more and more unstable and volatile. Generational feuds amongst powerful noble families polarized the nobles, causing further instability in political circles. Feuds like those of the Percy and Neville families added to the slow formation of the Civil War. Also, by this time, Richard of York was once more a major player of the opposition. When the situation reached a critical point, a Regency Council was established in order to ensure that the country could be governed during Henry VI's mental breakdown. And the leader of the Council was Richard of York, now the Lord Protector and Chief Councilor. Henry's wife, Margaret of Anjou was a staunch protestor of his position, but to no avail. What is more, Richard of York promptly placed Richard Neville, the Earl of Salisbury (his brother-in-law), at the prominent position of Chancellor, thus antagonizing their rivals in the Percy family. This gained him a powerful ally - the Neville family, most importantly Richard Neville, Earl of Warwick, who was at this time one of the richest and most powerful nobles in England. This was the crucial part of "setting up the stage" for the Wars of the Roses. By 1455, Henry VI made an unexpected recovery from his mental breakdown, and quickly reversed the changes that Richard of York had made. Subsequently, he forced him out of court and into exile. But by that point, it was too late - the "chess board" was all set up. The powerful displeased nobles - the powerful Earl of Warwick and his father Earl of Salisbury, or the Nevilles - quickly backed the claims of the House of York for control of the government. In response, Henry VI and Edmund Beaufort, the Duke of Somerset (the chief rival of Richard of York), decided to hold a Great Council at Leicester on May 22nd, where it was feared by the Yorkists that charges of treason would be brought against them. For this reason, Richard of York and his close supporters assembled an army, with which they planned to intercept the Royal part at St. Albans. The stage was set.

Chapter IV

What happened next was the first engagement of the Wars of the Roses, and a clash that is commonly used as the opening event of the war. Richard of York led a sizable army that ranged between 3,000 and 7,000 troops, while the King's party numbered just 2,000 troops and retainers. The latter party did not know of Richard of York's intentions and movements until it was too late, and they were already en-route to Leicester. Henry VI attempted to hastily assemble a matching army, but to no avail. On May 21st, 1455, the two armies were encamped during the night, just 20 miles apart from one another, and it became clear that an armed engagement could not be avoided. During the night, both sides decided to march towards the nearby city of St. Albans, where Henry VI arrived first at 7 am. The forces of Richard of York were halted nearby, at a position called Key Fields. Over the next three hours the two sides attempted a reconciliation, but to no avail. With Henry's side refusing to accept Richard of York's demands of surrendering Somerset, the First Battle of St. Albans ensued.

The Yorkist battle plan consisted of a devastating barrage of arrows loosened at the command of Earl of Warwick, which would in turn support two flanking attacks by Richard of York and Earl of Salisbury. However, the flank attacks were repulsed, and Warwick's archers had to focus on their own frontline before making a push and breaking through the Lancastrian center. This divided the latter's troops, and they had to fall back in order to avoid being outflanked. By doing so, historians agree that the Lancastrian army weakened their defenses within the city of St. Albans, allowing the Yorkist troops to press the advantage and swarm the city and its defenders. In the ensuing chaos, the Lancastrian army panicked and broke, turning to flight as it was being pursued by the victorious Yorkists. The battle was brief and ended as a decisive victory for the Yorkist party, with no more than 160 casualties on both sides.

However, the "spoils of battle" were much more significant. Some of the influential nobles that supported King Henry's side were slain in battle, and thus Richard of York quickly removed some of his staunch rivals and opponents. Notable dead were Thomas Clifford the 8th Baron of Clifford, Henry Percy the 2nd Earl of Northumberland, Edmund Beaufort the 2nd Duke of Somerset, and many other important knights and esquires. Beaufort died while conducting one last, desperate charge against his enemies. Within one of the buildings, the King, Henry VI, Duke of Buckingham, and the Earls of Dorset and Devon were hiding. It was there they were captured alive by the Yorkist troops. It is said that the King was hiding in a tanner's shop, abandoned by his closest supporters. Either way , the victory at St. Albans completely reversed the political situation in England, especially with the fact that Richard of York held the King prisoner and was rid of most of his staunch rivals. In October of that year, Richard of York was appointed Lord Protector by the Parliament, which helped the Yorkist faction to reach a position of influence once again. Warwick was also given a lofty position, being named the Captain of Calais, the city which coincidentally had the only standing army of the King. Such a position held great power, both militarily and elsewise, and the young Earl of Warwick was quickly able to rise in prominence thanks to his successful anti-piracy activities in the English Channel. In no time he became the staunchest ally of Richard of York.

Over the next three years, England stood on the brink of warfare, as a strenuous peace was barely kept afloat. In early 1456, Henry VI again regained his "mental faculties" and resumed personal governance of the realm: Richard of York lost his position as the Protector and returned to Ireland. This left the Earl of Warwick as the largest Yorkist threat to the Lancastrian court, behind which stood Margaret of Anjou, the King's wife. She repeatedly attempted to oust Warwick from his position of influence but was not successful. Warwick refused to surrender Calais, and kept it occupied as a major haven for Yorkist supporters.

By late 1458, the fragile peace slowly disintegrated into shambles. Henry was desperate to regain peace within his own realm, which was once again troubled by internal affairs, most notably the feud between the Percy and the Neville families. The Earl of Warwick also was a major threat, continually disregarding Lancastrian royal authority. He conducted several attacks within the channel and kept relations with the French leaders. Henry summoned him (and Richard of York) to London to be inquired about the attacks - a demand which Warwick and York refused outright, knowing that they would likely be arrested upon arrival. Instead of peace, the two opposing parties once again began arming and preparing for war in 1459. The Earl of Warwick departed Calais with a considerable army, attempting to join his forces with Richard. The latter was amassing troops in his powerful stronghold at Ludlow Castle. The Lancastrians likewise gathered troops and attracted supporters for Henry's cause, and soon enough, it came to blows once again.

The Battle of Blore Heath occurred on September 23rd, 1459, when the Lancastrian forces, numbering between 10,000 and 12,000 troops, attempted to ambush the Yorkist troops that numbered just 5,000. Their ambush didn't go as planned however, as the Yorkist scouts spotted them in due time. The Earl of Salisbury decided to stay his ground and give battle, which proved to be the right decision. Although outnumbered, the Yorkists decisively defeated the Lancastrian ambushers, causing some 2,000 casualties and killing the prominent Lancastrian leader, James Tuchet the Baron Audley.

However, in September, the Yorkist tasted defeat for the first time, this time at Ludford. This clash is known as the Rout at Ludford Bridge, and it was - for the most part - a bloodless engagement. However, the Calais troops that were under Warwick's command, and led by the professional soldier Andrew Trollope, defected and betrayed

Warwick in the critical moment. Due to this, the Yorkist faction was once again forced to scatter and flee. Richard of York was once again forced to flee to Ireland, while Warwick promptly sailed back to Calais where he managed to regain the loyalty of the garrison. Henry VI's court, on the other hand, assembled a Parliament whose purpose was to attaint their opponents - Richard of York and Earl of Warwick. This Parliament, however, caused many of the Lords who were uncommitted up to that point, to fear for their own titles and holdings.

By June 1460, Earl of Warwick returned to England with a force of 2,000 men. He landed at Sandwich and quickly amassed many supporters in the land who flocked to his cause. At this time, the King and his wife were at Coventry. Upon hearing the news of their enemy's landing, they hastily assembled an army and rushed south. But by July 2nd, Warwick entered London, his army now 5,000 strong. He quickly took London for his own, with only the Tower of London holding out for the King. The latter, hearing that the capital was now in Yorkist hands, ceased his march and took up a defensive position at Northampton, where he was to await further reinforcements.

Warwick left a small force to keep the Tower of London under siege, and he took the bulk of his army to meet the King in battle at Northampton. The Battle of Northampton was fought on July 10th, 1460, under heavy rain. What ensued was a critical battle. At first, the Yorkist troops had difficulties crossing the sodden terrain - they were decimated by heavy arrow barrage and could not fight in close quarters due to the protective stakes and earthworks that the Lancastrians put up. However, one critical event turned the tide of the battle. And that was the treachery of Baron Edmund Grey. When it seemed certain that the Yorkists would be routed, he held aloft a ragged badge of Earl of Warwick, signifying his loyalties, and ordering his men to lay down their weapons. Following this, Baron Grey's men switched sides and began helping Yorkist troops over the stakes and defenses. Butchery soon ensued, with Warwick's troops now essentially behind their enemies who were unable to maneuver in the tight quarters. In no time, the Lancastrians broke and fled in panic, with many prominent nobles dying at the field of battle. Among these were Humphrey Stafford the Duke of Buckingham, John Talbot the Earl of Shrewsbury, John Beaumont Viscount Beaumont, Thomas Percy, Lord Egremont, and others.

King Henry VI was once more captured alive and taken to London as a prisoner. Once there, he was forced to compel the Tower Garrison to surrender, and also to sanction a Yorkist government. Richard of York returned from Ireland and pressed his claims to the throne of England. He did so with a symbolic gesture of placing his hand on the throne, a thing forbidden to all. It is said that this seemingly simple (but highly controversial) gesture shocked the assembled peers, and even the closest supporters of Richard were not prepared for such a move. The judges and the peers rejected his claims, with many of the lesser nobles being uninterested in usurping King Henry from his throne, while the judges could not find a solution due to the uncommon situation with the succession. However, a compromise was achieved. It was known as the Act of Accord, passed on October 25th, 1460. It stated that in the case of Henry VI's death (the peers would not support Richard while Henry lived), Richard would be the next to succeed him at the throne, while Henry's son Edward would be disinherited. It was a fragile compromise at best and would soon prove to be completely unacceptable for either side. The conflict promptly resumed.

While King Henry VI was being captured at the Battle of Northampton, the Queen and their son Edward promptly fled - first to North Wales where they were joined by Jasper Tudor, then to the north. There, Margaret of Anjou began gathering supporters and forming a new army to face the Yorkists. Soon she "overran" Yorkshire and gathered new Lancastrian supporters from the West Country region. Richard of York, in the meantime, sent his own son, Edward the

Earl of March, to gather troops in the Welsh Marches, while he himself led the bulk of the Yorkist army northwards, to meet the Lancastrian troops in battle. What ensued was one of the most important clashes of the Wars of the Roses. On December 16th, 1460, Richard of York's army clashed with the Lancastrians at the Battle of Worksop. It was not a battle per se, but rather a skirmish, in which York's forces were allegedly defeated.

Following this defeat, York learned that Margaret's army was now positioned at Pontefract Castle. Thus, he promptly marched his own army to his personal stronghold of Sandal Castle, distanced just 9 miles from Pontefract and 2 miles from the city of Wakefield. At Sandal, Richard of York was essentially blockaded by the Lancastrians. Margaret's troops were now four times as numerous as his own, which made any prospect of battle impossible. He thus decided to wait in the castle and await reinforcements. What ensued next, on December 30th, is confusing for most historians. It is possible that the Lancastrians drew Richard into a well-orchestrated trap: a small part of their army began advancing on Sandal Castle as if assaulting, while two separate armies were positioned in the woods, flanking the open field of battle. It is likely that Richard of York thought that he was misinformed, and that the Lancastrian army was considerably smaller than previously thought. Thus, he led his army straight down the slope from Sandal Castle, attempting to break the main Lancastrian line. This he almost did, but oblivious to the threats on his flanks. In the critical moment, the ambush was sprung, and two heavy attacks obliterated the Yorkist army. It was a total decimation of the Yorkist army.

Historians to this day can't decisively answer why did Richard of York sortie from his safe position. Was it rashness, miscalculation, or deception? We might never know. Either way, Richard of York, the main opponent of the Lancastrian King, Henry VI, was killed in the mayhem. Some say that he was captured alive, given a mock crown made of bulrushes, and then promptly beheaded. Those who died by his side were the chief Yorkist nobles: Richard's son Edmund was dead; as were Sir John and Hugh Mortimer, Richard Neville the Earl of Salisbury and his son Thomas Neville, William Lord Harrington, and many others.

Chapter V

With the death of Richard of York, one would think that the Yorkist cause was all but extinguished. To be sure, it was a devastating blow for the Yorkist faction as a whole - but his death was certainly not enough to put an end to it. The Earl of Warwick was still alive in London and a major threat, as was Richard's son, Edward - now the new Duke of York. The former was still in London, and the latter was in the Welsh Marches, gathering supporters. The two, although devastated by the news of Richard's demise, were still busy gathering new Yorkist armies. In the Welsh Marches particularly, followers gathered around Edward, wishing to avenge their fallen lords and knights that fell at Wakefield. And just a month after that fated battle, Edward now commanded a considerable force that was based at Hereford.

By January 1461, Edward set out on a march that would unite his forces with Warwick's, so that together they could intercept the Queen's army before it reached London. However, as soon as he started off, he learned of two new Lancastrian forces on the march: those of Earls of Wiltshire and Pembroke. This placed him in a bad position, where he could be easily trapped between two major Lancastrian armies. Due to this, Edward decided to shift 17 miles to the north, to a place called Mortimer's Cross, near Ludlow. Here was a river crossing over the River Lugg, and the crossroads of two critical roadways. Here, Edward deployed his armies on February 2nd, 1461. And soon enough, the Lancastrian armies arrived at the same place, also deploying for the inevitable battle. By noon of that day, they began to march directly against the main Yorkist line. What ensued was the ferocious Battle of Mortimer's Cross, which was an exciting engagement full of unexpected turns.

The general layout of the battle presents three distinct "battles", i.e., armies, facing off against one another. On the right flank, Yorkist troops were overcome and pushed back by the "battle" of James Butler,

Earl of Wiltshire and Ormond. However, at the very same time, the main force of Edward Duke of York completely devastated the central force of Jasper Tudor, the Earl of Pembroke. Seeing this, Earl of Ormond shifted his troops towards the center in order to support the main fighting force, but seeing that he was already crushed, he decided to halt his troops and rest, waiting to see the result of the combat on the extreme flank. The reason for this illogical decision is still debated, many centuries later. Either way, the force of Owen Tudor was on the leftmost flank, and made attempts to outflank the Yorkist troops. It was a foolish move, to say the least. By committing to a flanking maneuver, Tudor completely exposed his own left flank to the waiting Yorkist troops. The latter seized the chance that was offered as if on a silver platter: they made a vicious charge into the Lancastrian side, cutting their formations in half and causing them to flee. Soon after, it was all over: the Lancastrian armies turned into an all-out panicked retreat and were pursued by the Yorkists and cut down en masse. Before the actual battle began, a curious event occurred. It is known in professional terms as a "parhelion": a natural, meteorological phenomenon in which the sun appears to be threefold. The Yorkist troops were generally alarmed and frightened by this unbelievable sight of "three suns arising". However, Edward cunningly explained to them that it was in fact a "sign from God", and that the three suns symbolized the Holy Trinity. He claimed that God was on their side and thus sent them a sign. The morale of the troops was greatly bolstered by this. Following the battle, Edward took for his personal sigil the heraldic symbol of such a sun, which was known as the "Sunne in Splendour".

A foremost casualty of this battle was Sir Owen Tudor, the second husband of Catherine of Valois, the widow of Henry V. He was captured after the battle and thought that he would be imprisoned. His captors, however, had no intention of doing that. When he realized he was going to be killed, Tudor reportedly said:

"that hede shalle ly on the stocke that wass wonte to ly on Quene Katheryns lappe." ("That head shall lie on the stock, that was wont to lie on Queen Catherine's lap.")

He was promptly beheaded, and his head placed unceremoniously on the market cross at Hereford. There it is said:

"that a *madde woman kembyd hys here and wysche a way the blode of hys face"* (*"a mad woman combed his hair and washed away the blood on his face"*),

and then lit 100 candles all around him. Mortimer's Cross was a major Yorkist victory in the Wars of the Roses.

In the meantime, Queen Margaret's armies marched southwards to London. In her ranks were many Scottish and Welsh borderers and mercenaries, eager to pillage and wage war. And true enough, these mercenaries pillaged all along their march, leaving ruin and despair wherever they ventured. This was due to the fact that Margaret could not pay her soldiers, and thus promised a bountiful pillage of London itself and of South England, also. Within London, the Earl of Warwick waited. He had a lack of men at his disposal, and the defense of the city seemed impossible. However, as soon as Edward won at Mortimer's Cross, the situation changed. Men joined Warwick's cause, bolstered by the news of the victory, and the earl was soon at the head of a considerable army. On the 12th of February 1461, he marched out of the capital to intercept Margaret, urging Edward to join up with him as soon as possible. The place that Warwick chose for the battle was already blood-soaked. It was the site of the First Battle of St. Albans. Once more, Warwick prepared defensive positions along a 3-mile front, barring the path to London at St. Albans. However, the forces of Margaret were not so easily swayed. Moving south, the Queen first shifted her movements to the south-west, apparently in an attempt to prevent the joining of forces of Edward and the Earl of Warwick.

Next up, she managed to receive news of Warwick's deployments at St. Albans. Because of this, she marched her troops south-west past Luton, from where she swung towards St. Albans from the west, attempting to decisively turn Warwick's defensive positions. Queen Margaret's borderer troops continued to pillage the countryside elsewhere, diverting the Yorkist attention there. By February 16th, Margaret's troops arrived at the forward Yorkist positions at Dunstable, where they surprised them, and killed and captured every single man there. Throughout the entire night, she marched her army to St. Albans. On February 17th, her troops were in position and the battle began. The Yorkists were again taken by surprise but managed to defend themselves within the town proper.

The Earl of Warwick found himself in a difficult position now. By 10 am, the town of St. Albans was in Lancastrian hands, and King Henry VI was found in a house there and freed from captivity. Warwick now had to rearrange his positions, since his defensive line was all but useless. The battle then turned to utter failure for the Yorkists. Warwick had difficulties reorganizing his troops and forming new lines, especially after morale was shaken with the desertion of a major detachment under Sir Henry Lovelace, Warwick's own steward who defected over to the Lancastrians. Somehow, Warwick assembled a new defensive position and managed to stave off further Lancastrian attacks until the dark, when he extricated 4,000 of his men and retreated westwards in an attempt to join forces with Edward. The Second Battle of St. Albans was an important Lancastrian victory, made possible through shrewd maneuvering and outwitting of Warwick. But most importantly, it resulted in the freeing of King Henry VI, which once again turned the tables. But the Earl of Warwick, now popularly called "the Kingmaker", was a man of absolute ambition and perseverance: Second St. Albans was not enough to deter him.

Queen Margaret marched to London, only to find its gates barred to her and Henry. The citizens were in full panic mode due to the pillaging behavior of the Lancastrian troops, and refused to let them in. As a result, the Scots and Welsh borderers deserted the Lancastrian army in great numbers, an event that forced Margaret to abandon her claim to London and to march to York instead. And so it was that just 12 days after their defeat at St. Albans, the Yorkists - Edward and Warwick now united - entered London triumphantly. There, with the full support of his Yorkist peers, Edward the Duke of York was proclaimed as King Edward IV. Now, with a united army, the Yorkists continued their pursuit of Henry VI, on March 19th. On March 27th, the advance Yorkist guard was staved off at Ferrybridge by a delaying force of the Lancastrians, but this did not prevent their march from continuing. Throughout the entire next day, they pushed back the Lancastrian troops towards Towton. There, the Queen's army waited in battle formations. What resulted was one of the bloodiest battles ever fought on the English soil: the Battle of Towton.

The Battle of Towton was fought on March 29th, 1461, under heavy snowfall in an almost fantastical ambience. The two armies, together numbering roughly 60,000 men, advanced towards each other in what was a true "duel of the fates". When they were about 300 yards apart, the Yorkist troops halted and promptly let loose a devastating volley of brutal, armor piercing arrows. This volley caused moderate casualties amongst the Lancastrians. The latter, however, responded in equal measure, but oddly enough with lighter, short-range arrows. Due to the wind, these arrows fell short of their mark, and soon the Lancastrian archers emptied their quivers without causing any considerable damage to their opponent. The Yorkist archers seized this chance to close in and again discharge a devastating volley of heavy arrows. Seeing that they would be decimated if stationary, the Lancastrian troops abandoned the arrows exchange and marched to close the distance as quickly as possible. Soon after, swords and spears clashed with a deafening clank of steel on steel. The battle was fought throughout the day, with casualties mounting on both sides. No complex maneuvers, no larger-than-life events: just two battle lines hacking away at one another until the last man standing.

Around 3pm on that day, the seasoned Lancastrian commander, Lord Dacres, fell in battle. It was said that he was struck by an arrow from an archer hiding in a tree canopy. Either way, his death shaken the morale of the Lancastrians. This was made worse with the arrival of John Mowbray, 2nd Duke of Norfolk, who reinforced the Yorkists with a force of several thousand men. He struck to the flank and caused widespread panic amongst the Lancastrians, who by that point suffered heavy losses. In no time, the whole Lancastrian line of battle collapsed, and they turned to a panicked rout. Men fled in all directions, running across the fields where the pursuing Yorkists cut them down en masse. Before the battle, both sides gave an order of "no quarter", which meant no mercy and no prisoners. Many of the Lancastrian soldiers, knights, and nobles who gave up were simply executed on the spot. Others fell as they ran. Some drowned in the nearby river, unable to cross it with ease. Either way, it was a true massacre. It is said that more Lancastrians died while fleeing than while fighting. It was unarguably the bloodiest battle ever fought on English soil: some estimates propose roughly 20,000 Lancastrians killed, and 8,000 to 12,000 thousand dead Yorkists.

Over the centuries, historians offered different numbers of casualties, some smaller and more reasonable, but either way - the numbers were appallingly high. Amongst the dead Lancastrians were numerous chief nobles and supporters of their cause, notably Lord Dacres; Sir Andrew Trollope with his son and heir Sir David Trollope; Henry Percy the Earl of Northumberland; Lord Lionel de Welles, Baron Welles; Lord Ralph Bigod, Baron Mauley; Thomas Courtenay Earl of Devon; James Butler, Earl of Ormond and Wiltshire, and many others. The death of the career soldier, Sir Andrew Trollope, was seen as a major blow for the Lancastrian cause, since the man was a seasoned commander of their armies and a capable warrior.

Modern archeological excavations of the site revealed a mass grave with many badly damaged skeletons. It is believed that this was the site of burial of many of the battle's casualties. Examinations revealed that many of these skeletons had vicious wounds, many to their backs, necks, heads, and upper torso, which is indicative of wounds inflicted while they were on the run. It was carnage - through and through. But such carnage was perhaps needed in the Wars of the Roses, in order to determine the prevalence of either Yorkist or Lancastrian cause.

Either way, the victory at Towton firmly solidified the claims of Edward IV, confirming his kingship. It was one of the most decisive victories of the entire conflict. Following such a dreadful defeat, the Lancastrians broke. King Henry VI and his Queen Margaret, together with their young son Edward, fled to Scotland into exile. On the other hand, Edward fulfilled the original goals of his late father. And the people of England liked him, too. He was described as popular and likeable. Furthermore, contemporary accounts, such as those of Philippe De Commines, describe him as energetic, affable, and rather handsome. Being some 195 centimeters high (which was uncommon for the time), he was an imposing and striking figure, especially when in the saddle and dressed in fine livery or exquisite armor. His advisors went to great lengths to make him seem as powerful and lively as possible, in order for him to be the stark opposite of Henry VI, who was seen by all as feeble, humble, and mentally frail. In short: Edward had all the prerequisites for kingship.

The early years of his reign were marked with an effort to stamp out all and any remaining Lancastrian opposition which was a threat to his rule. The Earl of Warwick remained in the north to subdue remnants of opposition, while King Edward IV attainted 14 leading Lancastrian peers that lived still, and some 96 knights and minor nobles. However, the remaining Lancastrians retreated north to Scotland alongside their deposed King Henry VI, where they sought refuge and assistance from the Scots. In the meantime, on the 28th of June 1461, Edward was formally crowned in Westminster Abbey as King Edward IV. He was the first Yorkist King of England.

Still, Edward later sought to win over his defeated enemies, especially those who chose to submit to his rule. Many of the Lancastrians he attainted were pardoned after submitting to him and allowed to retain all their titles and holdings. Needless to say, the one who benefited the most was none other than Richard Neville, Earl of Warwick, popularly called the "Kingmaker". Thanks to his support for the new king, he was made the wealthiest and most powerful noble in England, becoming the Steward of the Duchy of Lancaster, the High Admiral of England, Captain of Calais, alongside being Baron Monthermer, Earl of Salisbury, and Baron Montagu. After the King, he was the second richest man in the realm. He continued to be a valuable asset of the Yorkist cause, especially after successfully negotiating a truce with Scotland in 1462.

Sporadic conflicts with the Lancastrians continued at a steady pace, first in Ireland, and then in October 1462 when Margaret employed troops from France to invade England. Her forces captured the English castles of Bamburgh and Alnwick but could not hold them for long - losing them after three months. In early 1463, the North revolted, supporting the Lancastrian cause when Sir Ralph Percy, a noted Lancastrian, laid siege to Norham Castle in Northumberland. Little came out of this, as Warwick regained the lost territories in the north by the following year. However, in April 1464, hostilities resumed in earnest. In that month, the two parties skirmished at Hedgeley Moor, where Sir Ralph Percy stood his ground and was annihilated and killed.

Following this, a new major clash unfolded: the Battle of Hexham. It was fought on May 15th, 1464, when the main Lancastrian army, moving south through Northumberland, met and clashed with the Yorkist army under the leadership of John Neville, 1st Marquess of

Montagu, the younger brother of Warwick the "Kingmaker." In the early morning, Lord Montagu ordered the attack of his Yorkist troops from a favorable position: his troops were in a downhill charge which gave them momentum. Such a devastating charge destroyed the Lancastrian positions and ended in a decisive Yorkist victory. At Hexham, most of the leading remaining Lancastrian nobles were captured, notably Henry Beaufort, 3rd Duke of Somerset, Baron Hungerford, and Baron Ros. All three were summarily executed. Their deaths virtually completed the extinction of the old Lancastrian faction, severely hindering all Lancastrian resistance and their cause. Queen Margaret fled to France after this, while King Henry VI, who was present at Hexham, fled northwards. He spent some time hiding amongst his supporters, in houses, manors and castles, avoiding capture. He was tracked down to Waddington in Lancashire, where he was hiding in the manor of Sir Richard Tempest, in Waddington Hall. Records say that Henry was betrayed by a monk. He ran to the nearby woods, but the Yorkist men captured him, and he soon ended up imprisoned in the Tower of London. His capture almost extinguished the Lancastrian cause and all opposition to Edward's rule. However, King Edward saw no point in killing Henry VI. His young son Edward was still alive and free, as was his queen. He instead chose to keep Henry imprisoned, and with him, the Lancastrian cause. Henry's wife and their heir fled from Scotland to France, where they remained in the French court for many years, impoverished and disillusioned.

With all this set into motion, Edward IV was able to focus on his own goals and affairs of the court. And marriage was one of the foremost topics at hand. Edward knew that he would have to marry for an alliance: he wished that it be an alliance with the Duchy of Burgundy. However, the Earl of Warwick urged him to pursue an alliance with the French King, Louis XI. However, Edward opted for neither of these options. What ensued was a true and unprecedented incident, coming as a shock to many. Because Edward IV secretly married one Elizabeth Woodville on May 1st, 1464. The woman was a widow of a minor Lancastrian noble, herself coming from a minor noble house of landed gentry. However, she had the reputation of being the *"the most beautiful woman in the Island of Britain"*. For the Earl of Warwick, this was hard to believe. He was shocked, embarrassed, and full of rage since he felt betrayed and disregarded. Of course, Edward's secret marriage revealed to many that Warwick was not actually the power behind the throne, as many suspected. Furthermore, the marriage at once made the Woodville family rich and prominent, which they weren't, up to that point. In fact, the new Queen, Elizabeth, had 12 siblings, many of them married into other, more important noble families. The marriage made them all powerful political players that were largely out of control of Warwick the Kingmaker. Warwick was not the only one to criticize Edward's choice of bride: his Privy of Counselors also objected, stating that a man of royal blood such as he, should not marry a woman that was not a daughter of either a duke or an earl, at least. In short, the controversial marriage brought disruption to Edward's court, especially between him and his chief supporter, the Earl of Warwick. The latter at once attempted to depose the Woodvilles and to restore his lost influence by accusing Elizabeth and her mother of practicing witchcraft. His plan did not succeed.

Either way, this unsanctioned marriage was a true conundrum and created many troubles for Edward, unbeknownst to him at the time. He was accused of intentionally deceiving the French with negotiations of marriage to which he was never truly committed. Furthermore, he created more instability at court by placing Elizabeth's siblings and cousins - who were up to that point minor and unimportant gentry - into high and important positions at court. For example, he made his new father-in-law, Richard Woodville, into the new Earl Rivers, and the new Lord High Treasurer. It was an unprecedented move. Edward also made another secret treaty with Burgundy in October

1466, again without the knowledge of Warwick. The latter was left to lead negotiations with France, without knowing that they were absolutely impossible at that point. And believe it or not, Edward continued his streak of unpopular decisions, further antagonizing his chief ally - Warwick the Kingmaker. In 1467 he removed Warwick's brother the Archbishop of York, from his prominent position of Lord Chancellor, and then refused to marry his brother, George, the Duke of Clarence, to Warwick's eldest daughter Isabel. Such a marriage would, in some small way, give Warwick's daughter the pretensions to the throne. And he just continued showering his new in-laws with prominent titles: his brother-in-law became Lord Scales, while Elizabeth Woodville's son from her first marriage became Earl of Dorset. This made them immensely rich virtually overnight. Some old supporters were also promoted: Humphrey Stafford became the 1st Earl of Devon, William Herbert was made the Earl of Pembroke, while the Percys were restored to their Earldom of Northumberland. The Percy family, as we said, were the foremost enemies of the Neville's, the family to which the Earl of Warwick belonged. Needless to say, all of this greatly alienated Warwick the Kingmaker, who was up to Edward's coronation his chief and most loyal ally, and - in many ways - the one responsible for his military successes. Such actions in the English court only spelled doom for the hard gained positions of the Yorkist faction.

Around April 1459, things took a turn for the worse. In Yorkshire, a popular rebellion erupted, led by an enigmatic figure that was known as Robin of Redesdale. Some said, however, that it was a pseudonym for Sir John Conyers, the steward of Middleham and a long-time loyal retainer and supporter of Richard Neville, the Earl of Warwick. Thus, it is supposed that the revolt was actually instigated by Warwick as a plan to depose King Edward from his throne. Further suspicions arose after the Nevilles made little to no attempts to quell the revolt. History tells us that Warwick did in fact have such plans. He allied himself with George of Clarence, the brother of Edward IV, who was supposed to be married to Isabel, Warwick's daughter. The two departed to Calais, where the latter declared himself *against* King Edward IV because of his "bad counselors" and his oppressions. Up to that point, they used the pretense of suppressing "Robin of Redesdale's Revolt" to gather troops and armies of their own. When in Calais, Warwick orchestrated a secret ceremony in which George of Clarence and Isabel Neville were married.

When the time was right, and the revolt of Redesdale was well under way, Warwick the Kingmaker sailed over from Calais and landed in Kent, ready for war. His goals were to "remove the evil counselors" from the company of the King, and to reinstate good governance of the realm. However, his true, private aims were much simpler to deduce. He wanted to depose Edward from the throne and to install George of Clarence instead.

As was predicted by many, Warwick moved his army northwards in an attempt to link-up with the rebels of Redesdale. However, before the two could link up, Redesdale already clashed with the Royal Yorkist troops. This was the Battle of Edgcote Moor, fought on July 24th, 1469. It unfolded in a tranquil vale that stretches near the Cherwell River. Yorkist Welsh armies under Black William Herbert, Earl of Pembroke, and under Sir Humphrey Stafford the Earl of Devon, moved northwards in order to support King Edward IV at Northampton, in his struggle against Redesdale's rebels. However, Redesdale himself, with an army up to 5,000 men strong, intercepted while moving south to join up with Warwick the Kingmaker. The two armies inevitably clashed in battle. After a prolonged struggle , the rebels won a decisive victory. For the Royalists (Yorkists), and especially for the Welsh troops of Pembroke, this was a devastating defeat and a major setback. Casualties amongst the Welsh troops ran to 2,000, while 168 Welsh noblemen, knights, and gentry were killed in the field of battle. Furthermore, the Earl of Pembroke himself was dead: he was captured and executed in Northampton. His own brother, the prominent Welsh noble, Sir Richard Herbert was also executed, as was their half-brother Sir Richard Vaughan. Sir Humphrey Stafford the Earl of Devon was captured and later lynched by an angry mob and beheaded. It was a devastating loss of nobility for the Yorkist cause. It was also eulogized by Welsh bards and poets for more than a century later.

The victory at Edgcote Moor temporarily shifted the balance of power in the realm in favor of Warwick the Kingmaker. Soon after the battle, King Edward IV was captured and held imprisoned at Middleham Castle. Warwick at once set about removing the upstart Woodvilles: on August 12th, 1469, after a mock trial, Sir Richard Woodville the Earl Rivers (father of Elizabeth Woodville, the Queen), and his son, John Woodville, were both beheaded at Kenilworth. Their heads were placed on spikes, above the gates of Coventry. However, it was soon clear that neither George of Clarence nor the Earl of Warwick enjoyed enough support in the realm to continue with their plan. After being confined for several weeks at Middleham, Edward IV was released back to the throne, after agreeing to accept several new ministers which Warwick proposed. However, the situation was not remedied: Edward could no longer trust Warwick and was bound to take his revenge.

In March 1470, a new revolt arose. This time, it was a Lancastrian uprising in Lincolnshire. However, it was likely induced by Warwick and Clarence after exploiting the political instability in the realm. They hoped to lure Edward with an army to the north, where they could capture him. The King, however, carefully surrounded himself with nobles who were against Warwick. With them, he marched to battle, and was victorious on March 12th, 1470, at the Battle of Losecoat Field. Here, Edward faced the rebellious forces led by Baron Willoughby, and proceeded to win a decisive victory. Before being executed, the captive Willoughby stated that Warwick and Clarence, were - as suspected - "partners and chief provokers" of the rebellion, and that it was all a plot to make George of Clarence the new King. This was all that Edward wanted to know. Warwick and Clarence promptly fled to France, in May of that year. There, they came in contact with the French King, Louis XI. The latter was quick to seize the potential of the English conflict, and to capitalize it to his own favor. Due to this, he arranged a reconciliation between Warwick the Kingmaker and his ex-enemy, Margaret of Anjou. The objective was to restore Henry VI to the throne, and Warwick was now - paradoxically - a Lancastrian supporter and, technically, switched sides. One of the many details of this arrangement was the marriage of Warwick's daughter Anne to Henry VI's son, Edward.

Following his change of sides, Warwick now orchestrated another uprising, this time in Yorkshire. When the revolt was in motion, he and Clarence set sail and landed in Dartmouth and Plymouth on September 13th, 1470, at the head of a small army. Many embittered followers quickly joined their cause. The first was Warwick's own brother, John Neville, the Marquess of Montagu, who resented the king and the loss of his earldom. The whole of Devon rose to Warwick's cause, and Kent followed suit. London too joined him, opening its gates to his troops. Edward was somewhat taken by surprise. His options were now limited, and he hurried south to meet the invading forces. However, he now faced the threat of Warwick from the south, and the Marquess of Montagu from the north. In many ways, he was encircled. With his troops dwindling rapidly, he saw that there was no viable solution, so he "jumped ship" and fled to Flanders on October 2nd, together with his brother, Duke of Gloucester, and several hundred chief retainers and allies.

After this event, Henry VI was officially restored to the throne. And now everyone knew, with zero doubts, that Warwick the Kingmaker, his nickname duly deserved, was the effective power behind the throne. Margaret of Anjou, however, was not so trusting of Warwick, and refused to leave France, keeping her young son Edward of Westminster with her. In the meantime, the new royal court of Henry was somewhat unstable. Many of the chief lords distrusted Warwick and held him responsible for many of their kindreds' deaths in the preceding years. The disputes and distrust left Warwick and Clarence "politically isolated". Edward, however, did not lose time. In Flanders, he was received by the husband of his own sister, Charles the Bod, the ruler of Burgundy. Charles lent Edward some minor - but still precious - support in the form of some 1,500 German and Flemish mercenaries. With this force, Edward set sail back home and landed at Ravenspurn in Yorkshire on March 14th, 1471. He swiftly marched southwards, all the while skillfully evading an enemy army led by the Earl of Northumberland. Once he arrived at Nottingham, he received news of an army that Warwick was gathering at Coventry. As he continued on his way, Edward IV attracted many supporters to his cause. After he was joined by Sir William Parr and Sir James Harrington, together with their troops, his brother, George of Clarence, was now sufficiently convinced to abandon the Earl of Warwick. A major reason for this switching of sides was his political disadvantage amongst the Lancastrians. Seeing that Warwick's cause was unstable and weak, he quickly "abandoned ship" and went over to Edward, together with a considerable force that he gathered. Altogether, leading a formidable army, Edward and his allies reached London on April 11th, and quickly had Henry VI captured and imprisoned in the Tower of London.

In the meantime, Warwick was in an increasingly worsening situation: bad weather prevented Margaret of Anjou from sending over troops from France, and the defection of George of Clarence left his existing army much weaker. Either way, Warwick the Kingmaker marched in pursuit of Edward, and their two armies decisively clashed at the Battle of Barnet on April 14th, 1471. This was one of the culminating engagements of this period of the Wars of the Roses, and certainly shifted the narrative of things. The Battle of Barnet was marked by a difficult situation, due to the heavy fog that was present that morning. The battle began at dawn, and involved up to 45,000 men in total, on both sides. The formations started in two parallel lines, and the right wing of each of the two armies overcame the left wing of the other, in a sort of circular motion. On the Yorkist (Edward's) side, the Duke of Gloucester swung to the enemy's left flank, while on the Lancastrian (Warwick's) side, this was done by the Earl of Oxford. Both of the left flanks of each army were defeated. Soon after, both armies changed their positions, all the while hampered with poor visibility. At one point in the battle, the Lancastrian formations led by Oxford mistakenly attacked their own men of the center formations. The reason for this was certainly the thick fog that limited vision. Because of this, Lancastrian casualties mounted - from friendly fire. With the two friendly forces hacking away at one another, confusion arose. When realization of what was happening set in, it was quickly believed that treachery was at hand, and that Oxford had defected to the Yorkist cause and was thus attacking the Lancastrian center. As cries of treason sounded across the battlefield, many Lancastrians began deserting the battle in panic. At this moment, Edward IV launched a decisive cavalry charge that landed between Warwick and Somerset and quickly overwhelmed them. What ensued was a slow breaking of Warwick's forces, followed by an all-out panicked rout.

"Amidst howls of pain and rage, the troops that Oxford had rallied shouted 'Treason', believing that Warwick's men had changed sides as had happened with other lords in the climate of the times. Some, no doubt, shot arrows back, others decided the day must be lost if many of their own side had gone over to the enemy, and fled the field, according to Warkworth's Chronicle, taking some 800 men from the battle. As shouts of betrayal ran through the Lancastrian ranks, unease spread. In the thick mist the soldiers could not see what was happening further down the lines; in such conditions any cry of treason must have been deeply unsettling, especially as former enemies now fought on the same side. At

about the same time Gloucester pressed hard on Exeter's division in front and flank, slowly pushing them back. In the center Edward, who may have got an idea of the disarray in the enemy ranks, pressed the attack despite the damage to his left wing. [...] The enemy wavered and then broke."

It was a decisive Yorkist victory for Edward IV, and one that claimed some notable lives. First and foremost, to die in this battle was none other than Richard Neville, Earl of Warwick, the famed Kingmaker. During the final stages of the battle, he was cut down and killed. Sometime before him died his own brother, John Neville, the Marquess of Montagu. It was said that he fought most gallantly and bravely in this battle, and that he laid his life "in plain battle", in the thick of the fighting. "On the morrow after", the dead bodies of Montagu and Warwick were laid out, completely naked, in London's St. Paul Cathedral. This was done after direct orders from Edward, who wanted to quell any rumors that the two had somehow survived. Any citizen could openly observe their battle-mutilated corpses, *"laid in the church of Paul's, on the pavement, so that every man might see them; and so, they lay for three or four days".* After this "exhibition", Edward allowed the corpses to be buried with dignity at Bisham Priory, where many Neville's lay in eternal rest. With the deaths of Warwick, the Kingmaker and his brother, the Lancastrian cause suffered an immense blow. The Neville family also was irrevocably crushed with the death of their foremost representative, their political influence now cut to bits.

Alas, the Wars of the Roses was still on. The death of Warwick was not enough to put an end to things, as Henry VI still lived, as did his wife Margaret of Anjou and their boy, Edward of Westminster. On the very same day when the Battle of Barnet was fought, Queen Margaret and Prince Edward landed with their forces at Weymouth, where they were promptly joined with new recruits from the Welsh Marches. The Queen continued her march through the West Country, gathering men along the way, and heading towards Wales and the chief Lancastrian strongholds there. The survivors of Barnet, after fleeing the carnage, managed to rally around the newly arrived Queen. King Edward IV learned of her arrival, and quickly moved to intercept her and prevent the Lancastrians from reaching Wales. He conducted a series of rapid, forced marches in order to catch up with her as quickly as possible. He did so on May 3rd, at Tewkesbury.

The King's Demise

The very next day, May 4th, 1471, the two armies met on the battlefield, in the decisive Battle of Tewkesbury. The Lancastrians were greatly outnumbered here, and placed their army at a strong defensive spot, between two brooks and on a slope. Here, the Duke of Somerset, Edmund Beaufort, took the command of the right flank. He gave explicit orders to the commander of the central flank, Sir John Wenlock, Baron Wenlock, to support his flanking attack on Richard of Gloucester. As the battle erupted, Somerset launched his attack, but Wenlock hesitated and held back (some say on purpose), which resulted in Somerset's troops being decimated and defeated by Yorkist troops. In the heat of the battle, enraged by Wenlock's failure and indecisiveness, Somerset rode back from his defeated troops, approached Wenlock, and struck him in the head with his battle ax, killing him instantly. He blamed Wenlock's failure for the ultimate defeat in the battle. With Somerset's flank gone, the rest of the Lancastrian troops quickly faltered and then broke into a rout.

The Battle of Tewkesbury was a major Yorkist victory. It resulted in the death of some major Lancastrian figures. Most noted amongst these was the son of Henry VI, Edward of Westminster, who was just 17 years old at the time. Official accounts state that the young prince was discovered after the battle, grieving in a small grove. It was the men of the Duke of Clarence that discovered him, perhaps accompanied by the Duke himself. The young prince pleaded for his life, but to no avail: he was immediately beheaded on a makeshift block. Edmund Beaufort, the Duke of Somerset, the last male member of the Beaufort family, was captured and summarily executed after the battle. His own brother died as well. Also killed was the Earl of Devon. It was a true culling of Lancastrian nobility.

King Edward IV triumphantly returned to London, with the captive Queen Margaret of Anjou in tow. The lady was imprisoned in the Tower of London, where she remained for the next five years. That same evening, on May 21st, 1471, Henry VI died in his cell in the Tower of London. The official reports claim that Henry died from "melancholy", especially after learning of his son's death at Tewkesbury. However, this was far from the truth, and it was widely speculated that it was Edward IV who ordered his murder, or perhaps the Duke of Gloucester. Either way, Henry's death was inevitable, especially after his son and heir was executed. It was a sad, despondent end for Henry VI - the heir of brave Henry V of Monmouth - whose troubled reign was marked with mental illness and frailty.

Others prospered from the Lancastrian defeat. Edward quickly proclaimed his seven-month-old baby son as Edward, Prince of Wales, and was quick to put Calais under his own control. The bountiful lands and possessions of Earl of Warwick were passed on to Richard of Gloucester (Edward's brother) alongside his offices, while the Duke of Clarence (also Edward's brother) received the lands that belonged to the Courtenay family - alongside the position of Lieutenant of Ireland.

Following Tewkesbury, some sporadic attempts by Lancastrian supporters at continuing the fight appeared, but with no success. The Earl of Oxford, who previously fled to France, returned to England and landed at Essex and St. Michael's Mount. Here he attempted to raise an army and failed, subsequently surrendering in early 1474. With the decisive defeats at Barnet and then Tewkesbury, it seemed to all that there would not be any further armed Lancastrian resistance. However, internal feuds continued to mar the reign of Edward IV. Specifically, it was the constant feuding between his two brothers, the Duke of Clarence and the Duke of Gloucester. Things escalated in December 1476, when the wife of Clarence, Isabel (daughter of Warwick the Kingmaker), died. The Duke of Clarence, mourning his loss, accused late Isabel's lady-in-waiting, one Ankarette Twynyho, of murdering his wife. He was quick to murder that woman. This only deteriorated Clarence's relationship with his brother even further. The very next year, Duke of Clarence was proposed as a possible match for the new Duchess of Burgundy, Mary. Edward opposed this match, and Clarence left the royal court.

In 1475, Edward raised a great army with plans of invading France. He abandoned the entire expedition after signing the *Treaty of Picquigny* and receiving a substantial cash payment from the French. This allowed a degree of peace and prosperity to settle down onto England. It was only the constant quarreling with the Duke of Clarence that caused any degree of instability. He was dissatisfied with his position and did not hesitate to feud with both Edward and Richard of Gloucester. Things escalated in 1477 after some murders occurred which were carried out on Clarence's orders, as well with two uprisings - in Cambridgeshire and Huntingdonshire, which were suspectedly orchestrated by the Duke of Clarence. With widespread claims that Clarence was involved in a revolt against the King, Edward IV reacted and imprisoned Clarence in the Tower of London. The King had his brother accused of "unnatural, loathly treasons", which were only made worse because Clarence was his own brother - thus owing him loyalty and love. After a trial, George Plantagenet, the Duke of Clarence, was "privately executed" in the Tower of London (in Bowyer Tower), on February 18th, 1478. After the execution, rumors (likely the truth) arose that Clarence was drowned in a large barrel of Malmsey wine. He was just 28 years old at the time.

Chapter VI

In the later stages of his reign, King Edward IV was growingly frail and ill. At the time, medicine was still in infancy, and physicians of the court failed to find a logical reason for his illness. Some attributed it to Edward's frequent use of *emetics*, which allowed him to gorge himself at meals to no end, vomit everything out, and then return to eat anew. On Easter of 1483, Edward fell fatally ill, and it was clear that he would not recover. Hastily, he finished his will, and named his own brother, Richard of Gloucester, as Protector of the Realm after his death. Richard was to act as Lord Protector for Edward's young son and heir, the twelve-year-old Edward. On April 9th, 1483, King Edward IV died. Being acquired by such bloodshed and years of conflict, Edward's time at the throne of England was brief at best. Nevertheless, he brought a degree of stability and prosperity back to the nation.

Almost immediately after his death, trouble began brewing, as could be expected by that point. Rival factions emerged at once: one side was the faction of the boy-king, the supposed Edward V, and his own mother and their chief courtiers, Lord Hastings and Lord Stanley. On the other side, however, was the powerful Richard of Gloucester, the brother of the deceased king, and the most powerful magnate in the whole of England, and the explicitly named Lord Protector. Richard was urgently advised by his closest associates to bring a massive army to London in order to prevent any radical move that the upstart Woodville family (Queen's faction) might make. The tensions soared immensely in such a short time, as it was becoming obvious that the Woodvilles wanted to curb Richard's influence and perhaps make an attempt on his life. Queen Elizabeth Woodville instructed her brother, Earl Rivers, to promptly escort her son Edward V to London - alongside an armed escort of 2,000 men. Richard of Gloucester reacted accordingly, and on April 30th, 1483, he had the Earl Rivers, and several other nobles arrested and sent to the north, where they would not be a threat to him. He then swiftly moved southwards and seized the boy-king Edward V en route to London. The Queen Mother sought sanctuary within Westminster Abbey, while Richard placed his young nephews, sons of Edward IV, into the Tower of London. The boys were Edward V and his younger brother, the little boy Richard of Shrewsbury, Duke of York.

From the get-go, Richard, Duke of Gloucester, showed no mercy for his enemies. Despite his initial claims, he had Earl Rivers and his associates beheaded in June of 1483. With his powers as the legal Lord Protector, Richard continued to stall the coronation of young Edward V, despite being urged by his advisors to proceed with it. Everyone wanted to avoid another "protectorate" and the bloodshed that would inevitably come with it. Richard disregarded the urges and continued removing his chief enemies. On June 13th, he had the Lord Chamberlain, Baron Hastings, executed for treason - without trial. The death of Hastings was seen as a major controversy at the court, mainly due to the man's great popularity. Nevertheless, Richard knew that Hastings was a *major* obstacle towards his inevitable part to the throne. Make no mistake, Richard of Gloucester wanted to become the next English King. Soon enough, he took that next major step towards reaching his coveted goal.

In late June, Richard proclaimed that the marriage between Edward IV and Elizabeth Woodville was invalid, mainly because of Edward's prior union to one Eleanor Butler. This information he learned from Robert Stillington, the Bishop of Bath and Wells. Richard claimed that because of the invalidity of this union, young boy-king Edward V - as well as his siblings - was an illegitimate heir to the throne, a bastard. He proclaimed this at a sermon on June 22nd, which was taken as a date for Edward's official coronation. It was proclaimed that due to the boy being a bastard, it was in fact Richard of Gloucester who was the rightful king of the realm. The excited citizens urged him to take up that position. Four days later, Richard formally accepted the crown and was proclaimed King Richard III of England at Westminster Abbey on July 6th, 1483. Still, the heirs of Edward IV were a presence: the two boys were imprisoned in the Tower of London. However, by the late summer of 1483, they completely disappeared, and their fate remains a mystery to this very day. The subject is known as the "Princes in the Tower". By many, there is not a shred of doubt that the two boys were murdered on the orders of their powerful uncle, King Richard III. Leaving them alive would be too much of a threat for his reign, and it is most likely that he had them murdered soon after being crowned, in late 1483. Either way, the two boys were never seen again, after being imprisoned in the Tower of London. Many theories of their fate exist, and the question is still debated to this day. In 1674, during the remodeling of the Tower of London, workers dug out a wooden box that was buried some 3 meters (10 feet) beneath the staircase. Within it lay the bones of two children, one larger the other smaller, and many believed that they were the remains of the princes. However, bones of children were found before - and afterwards - within the Tower of London. On one occasion, before 1674, workers discovered an old chamber that had been walled up - and within it the bones of two children. The true, confirmed remains of the boys were never determined with certainty.

With Richard now the King of England, one would like to think that things would continue to prosper and take a turn for the better. But, knowing the history that precedes him, and the nature of the Wars of the Roses, peace was the furthest thing from reality. And so it was that in no time, hostilities once again resumed and threatened to engulf England fully and to continue the Wars of the Roses. The antagonized widow of Edward IV, Elizabeth Woodville, was still in the fight, and allied herself with Henry Stafford, 2nd Duke of Buckingham, a powerful disaffected magnate and the former ally of Richard III. Together, they joined up with Lady Margaret Beaufort, the lady who was actively promoting her own son, Henry Tudor the Earl of Richmond, as the new Lancastrian claimant to the throne. Henry Tudor was the great-great-great-grandson of Edward III, and the son of Edmund Tudor, the half-brother of late Henry VI. Moreover, Henry Tudor was seen as a viable alternative to King Richard III, and the closest living male heir to the Lancastrian claim to the throne. Elizabeth Woodville proposed to strengthen Tudor's claim to the throne by marrying him to her daughter, Elizabeth of York, the only living heir of Edward IV. This union attracted many Yorkist supporters to their cause, many of whom were eager to abandon Richard III, being a part of the disaffected gentry. By September of 1483, a conspiracy was being formed against Richard, mostly composed by the English nobles who were staunch supporters of Edward IV and his successors.

This early conspiracy was quickly and decisively crushed by Richard. Henry Tudor lived in exile at the court of Francis II, the Duke of Brittany. The Breton court saw them as valuable "guest-hostages", as the Duke Francis saw Henry Tudor as a powerful bargaining tool that would repeatedly gain him the English support in his conflicts with France. When the conspiracy against Richard began formulating, Duke Francis gave Henry Tudor his support in the form of a substantial payment of 40,000 gold crowns and some 15,000 troops. Tudor assembled a fleet that would sail him across the channel and to England, where he was to join up with the troops of the Duke of Buckingham. Alas, his fleet was scattered by a vicious storm, and he had to return back to France before he even started. However, the Duke of Buckingham already began the revolt, and was thus quickly crushed by the forces of Richard III, as he lacked crucial support from Henry Tudor. The Duke of Buckingham was captured and executed on November 2nd, 1483. Richard III's path towards removing his chief opponents was swift and brutal.

And so, as we can see, the Wars of the Roses showed no intent of halting. As soon as one monarch died, new pretenders to the throne came forth, each one staking his or her own claim. And with the swift rise of King Richard III, no prospect of peace was on the horizon in England. Because Henry Tudor pressed his claim.

After the failure of the Duke of Buckingham's unsupported revolt, the remaining supporters of Henry Tudor fled across the Channel to the capital of Brittany, Rennes. There, they flocked around Henry, gathering new forces. In the meantime, Richard III busied himself with negotiations with the Duke of Brittany, where he sought to win him over and get him to extradite Henry Tudor back to England. It was clear that the Duke of Brittany gave no particular support for Tudor's cause, but simply continued to refuse to extradite him in hopes of bargaining the best possible deal for himself. However, around 1484, the Duke of Brittany fell ill, giving the effective power of the Duchy to his official treasurer, Pierre Landais. This man was more pliant than the Duke, and Richard quickly reached an agreement for Tudor's extradition in exchange for English military support. Henry Tudor, however, gained word of this and promptly fled Brittany to the French court. There, at the court of King Charles VIII, he was received warmly, and received ample resources for his planned invasion of King Richard's realm. Charles VIII was likely eager to provide these resources as any instability within England certainly suited him.

In the first year of Richard's reign, a series of "ill-omens" occurred. In that year, his only legitimate child, his son and only heir, Edward of Middleham the Prince of Wales - died. The boy's death was sudden and unexpected, and dealt a heavy blow to Richard III's cause, as it deprived him of a legitimate heir to the throne that would continue the struggle. The boy was only ten at the time, and the parents were struck with maddening grief, as this contemporary excerpt tells us:

"However, in a short time after, it was fully seen how vain are the thoughts of a man who desires to establish his interests without the aid of God. For, in the following month of April, on a day not very far distant from the anniversary of king Edward, this only son of his, in whom all

the hopes of the royal succession, fortified with so many oaths, were centered, was seized with an illness of but short duration, and died at Middleham Castle, in the year of our Lord, 1484, being the first of the reign of the said king Richard. On hearing the news of this, at Nottingham, where they were then residing, you might have seen his father and mother in a state almost bordering on madness, by reason of their sudden grief."

Of course, Richard's enemies saw every misfortune that befell him as a direct sign from God. They believed that Richard was continuously being punished for the alleged murders of his own nephews, the young sons of Edward IV. In the next year, 1485, his own wife, Anne Neville (the daughter of the late Earl of Warwick), also died. The apparent cause of her death was tuberculosis, but many at the time believed that Richard III poisoned her in order to pursue a more influential marriage to solidify his reign. However, there exists no evidence to confirm this. In fact, contemporary accounts state that King Richard III wept at his wife's funeral and was stricken with grief. Nevertheless, the false rumors that circulated served only to alienate even more of his supporters. The situation was not helped by the fact that on the day that Anne Neville died, there was an eclipse in the skies. Richard's enemies took it as another sign from God.

In France, on the other hand, Henry Tudor - mostly with the help of his mother, Margaret of Beaufort - continued to gather support and to amass troops. On August 1st, feeling sufficiently prepared and eager to press his claim, he sailed over to England, bolstered by his Welsh, English, Scottish, and French troops. Soon after, he landed at Dale, in Pembrokeshire in Wales - the latter being his ancestral home. He conducted a swift march through the Welsh Marches, gathering further troops. Many Welshmen considered him as a sort of "messianic figure", and the leader who would defeat the "Saxons" and restore Wales to its former glory. In fact, several of Richard III's Welsh lieutenants defected from his cause and went over to Tudor. Nevertheless, King Richard III was adequately informed of Henry Tudor's movements, and continued mobilizing his troops and preparing for the inevitable confrontation. Many believed that the clash would be absolutely decisive and would decide the fate of the English throne. Soon enough, that fateful battle came to be on August 22nd, 1485, the forces of Henry Tudor and Richard III clashed in the famed Battle of Bosworth Field.

At Bosworth Field, near the town of Market Bosworth in Leicestershire, the two opposing armies drew up facing one another. However, one feature made battle uncommon: both Tudor and Richard III sought support from the forces of two brothers from the powerful noble family of Stanley. These were Sir William Stanley, and his brother Sir Thomas Stanley, the Earl of Derby. The Stanleys assembled their many troops upon hearing of Tudor's landing but did not officially declare their affiliation. They brought their forces to the battlefield at Bosworth, waiting at the sides and waiting to see which side it would be best to support. Neither Tudor nor Richard now knew who they would support, and they both anxiously looked on for their help. In the initial deployment stage, however, it was Richard III who had the numerical advantage.

As soon as the battle was underway, both sides sought to position themselves on the nearby Ambien Hill. It was Richard who reached it first and positioned his vanguard there in a defensive position. His main forces followed suit, while his rearguard under the Earl of Northumberland was ordered to take position to the left and face to the south. However, the rearguard never arrived at the position: the Earl of Northumberland decided not to engage and instead to wait and see what decision the Stanley brothers would make. As the two opposing armies now descended to a melee clash, the Stanleys showed "their hands." They swooped in like two ravenous vultures and attacked both flanks of Richard III's forces. All the while, the Earl of Northumberland remained inactive in place. Seeing that he had no support from Northumberland, King Richard III decided to take a great gamble and risk it all by taking his heavy knights and charging straight into the enemy center, where he hoped to kill Henry Tudor and swiftly end the battle - or die in the process. He conducted a glorious charge. However, when the Stanley brothers saw that Richard's cavalry was now separated from the main army, they swooped in and surrounded Richard's knights. Soon after, in the midst of a vicious fight, King Richard III was unhorsed and killed, overwhelmed by the superior numbers of the enemy. As soon as the news of his death rang out across the battlefield, the Battle of Bosworth Field officially came to an end. Many of Richard's troops fled and were not pursued.

The King in the Car Park

Richard III was the last English King to die on the field of battle. His death was widely regarded as heroic: even the personal historian of Henry Tudor wrote at the time that *"King Richard, alone, was killed fighting manfully in the thickest press of his enemies"*. To that end, there exist many contemporary accounts that describe the glorious conduct of Richard III in his final battle. It is said that during his brave charge, he fought gallantly, unhorsing a noted champion, Sir John Cheyne, and killing the standard bearer of Henry Tudor, Sir William Brandon. He then managed to come "within a sword's length" of Henry Tudor but was quickly surrounded by the troops of Sir William Stanley and killed. Of course, in the chaos of battle, it was hard to know who struck the deathly blow. Some contemporary sources stated that *"a Welshman struck the death blow with a halberd, while Richard's horse was stuck in the marshy ground"*. Many state that this Welshman was in fact *Rhys ap Thomas* (or one of his men), a leading Welsh knight and a prominent Lancastrian. Either way, the manner of Richard's death was truly violent. It was said that the blows were so vicious that the King's helmet was driven into his skull. After the battle, his naked body was tied to a horse and dragged to the nearby city of Leicester. Some early sources on the battle suggest that the body was displayed for all to see at the Church of the Annunciation of Our Lady of the Newark and was then buried - without any ceremony - at the Greyfriars Church in Leicester. Further sources state that in 1495, Henry Tudor - at that time the new King - paid a considerable sum of *£50 (equivalent to £42,013 in 2020)* for the erection of a marble and alabaster monument at the site. In more recent times, attempts were made at locating the resting place and the remains of King Richard III. However, the matter was considerably difficult: the Greyfriars Church in Leicester, known as his burial place, was long gone. During the period of the Dissolution of the Monasteries, the church was largely demolished, and in subsequent centuries, built over. A source states that in 1612 a marble memorial stone was still visible at the site, which was at the time a lush garden. Afterwards, as the wheels of time rolled on, the site of the Greyfriars Church - and the burial place of Richard III - were completely forgotten. No trace of it existed, owing to more than four centuries of development. However, archeologists set out on uncovering it in 2012, subsequently revealing the spot where Greyfriars Church once stood. In 2012, the spot was covered with streets and a car park. Nevertheless, on August 24th, 2012, it was announced by the University of Leicester and the Leicester City Council, that - together with the Richard III Society - a joint search would begin for the remains of King Richard III. The archeologists relied on old maps and accounts and historical sequences, and eventually managed to locate the remnants of the church beneath the earth. Its foundations still remained, buried beneath the modern-day city center of Leicester and the car park there. On September 5th, 2012, the archeologists announced the Greyfriars Church had been located. Just two days later, it was also announced that human remains - likely belonging to Richard III - were also found, buried beneath what was once the church's choir. Curiously, they were discovered beneath a large letter "R" painted on the tarmac of the car park, as if indicating an R for Richard. However, the "R", of course, indicated a reserved parking space, and the matter was just one of those mind-numbing coincidences that the universe so cunningly orchestrates. Either way, everything pointed to the fact that the skeleton was, in fact, that of King Richard III. Upon first glance, several key indicators confirmed this. The foremost was a severe scoliosis of the spine which likely made one shoulder higher than the other. And, truly so, King Richard III was known to have had this appearance aspect, and was called by his enemies as a "crookback" or "hunchback". Furthermore, the key indications were numerous wounds that the skeleton displayed: these were, for the most part, akin to wounds that Richard could have received. Most of the wounds were to the head, with also an arrowhead embedded in the spine. One of these wounds was caused by a rondel dagger, and another - a scooping depression in the back of the skull - caused by a sword. Closer examination showed that there were 11 wounds in total on the skeleton, of which 8 were to the skull. These wounds were made in battle, indicating that Richard lost his helmet at some point. Experts from the University of Leicester suggest that :

"The most likely injuries to have caused the king's death are the two to the inferior aspect of the skull—a large sharp force trauma possibly from a sword or staff weapon, such as a halberd or bill, and a penetrating injury from the tip of an edged weapon."

Still, there remained the matter of the skeleton's true identity. For that to be confirmed, a DNA test had to be made. But how do you find the DNA of a King that has been dead for centuries? In 2004, the noted British historian, John Ashdown-Hill, attempted to trace down matrilineal (through the mother's line) descendants of Anne of York, Duchess of Exeter, the elder sister of King Richard III. He managed to trace the lineage to a British woman that emigrated to Canada following the Second World War, one Joy Ibsen (nee Brown). She was, surprisingly, the 16th generation great-niece of King Richard, in the same maternal line. The son of Mrs. Joy Ibsen provided his DNA via a mouth swab in 2012. It was his mitochondrial DNA, passed down the direct maternal line, that was compared to the DNA of the skeleton and indeed confirmed that those were the remains of King Richard III. The King of England, who died in a glorious battle and lost his crown there, had - centuries later - become the King in the Car Park, resting beneath a large painted "R".

Chapter VII

The throne was now Henry Tudor's - won by conquest. As Richard III lay dead in the battlefield at Bosworth Field, the opportunist Lord Stanley bent down and took his royal circlet - the mark of his kingship. He then placed that circlet on the head of Henry Tudor, proclaiming him the new King of England - Henry VII. The new king was formally crowned on October 30th, 1485, in Westminster Abbey. His father was the half-brother of late Henry VI. He then proceeded to solidify his claim by marrying Elizabeth of York, the daughter of late King Edward IV. With this marriage, Tudor managed to unite the rival Lancastrian and Yorkist claims to the throne, because their offspring would then inherit the claims of both branches. Because of this, the Battle of Bosworth Field and the subsequent crowning of Henry Tudor can be seen as an effective end of the Wars of the Roses, but this can be a bit hasty since troubles still threatened the early days of Tudor's rule. First and foremost was the all too real "paranoia," a fear that anyone with a drop of Plantagenet blood was secretly wishing to be King and would burst out to press their claim. And, of course, as with most other new kings of the period, unhappy and rebellious nobles quickly stepped forward to challenge his reign. In the very same year of his coronation, he faced a revolt by the notable noble Stafford brothers and their ally Viscount Lovell. Their revolt, however, did not gain momentum and failed before any fighting was done.

In 1486, there erupted a rising in the North Riding of Yorkshire, a region where there were many supporters of late Richard III. The previously defeated Lovell now returned from his exile in Flanders and landed in Ireland, bringing some 2,000 Swiss and 1,500 German mercenaries, both of which were supplied by his ally in mainland Europe, Margaret of Burgundy. This force was now joined by a major player: John de la Pole, 1st Earl of Lincoln. Together with some 200 other noted Yorkists, John de la Pole, led the new rebellion in the name of a new Yorkist candidate for the throne, Edward the Earl of Warwick, the son of late George Plantagenet, Duke of Clarence (brother of Edward IV and Richard III). However, the boy Warwick was already imprisoned by Henry Tudor and kept in the tower of London. Because of this, the Earl of Lincoln found a "double," one Lambert Simnel, a boy of ordinary, humble origins who likely just had the same appearance as young Warwick. The Earl of Lincoln aimed to plant him on the throne, perhaps until the real Earl of Warwick could be released from London. Some suggest that Lincoln wanted the throne ultimately for himself, as he too had Plantagenet ancestry, being Richard III's nephew.

Either way, the new revolt found much support in Ireland, especially amongst the disaffected nobles there. The "false pretender" Lambert Simnel - his real identity unknown - was crowned on May 24th, 1487, at Christ Church Cathedral in Dublin as King Edward VI of England, a new Yorkist claimant to the throne. Still, Earl of Lincoln knew that this common boy was just a focal point of a needed Yorkist rebellion. One account tells us that:

"He [Lambert Simnel] was merely a commonplace tool to be used for important ends, and the attempt to overthrow Henry VII would have taken place had Simnel never existed. The Yorkist leaders were determined on a serious push, rising of their party in England supported by as great a force as possible from overseas."

Still, the new Yorkist revolt was now well under way. Lincoln's troops now recruited an additional four or five thousand Irish troops commanded by Thomas Fitzgerald. This was mostly possible due to overwhelming support of Gerald FitzGerald, 8th Earl of Kildare, a powerful Irish noble who benefited greatly from the previous Yorkist regime.

Now at the head of a considerable army, the Earl of Lincoln and other leaders of the rebellion sailed over to England and landed at Piel Island in Lancashire. The rebel army then continued on towards

York, a traditional stronghold of all Yorkist support. Oddly enough, however, Lincoln found no support for his cause there, and the town refused to open its gates to him. At this time, the Lancastrian royal army closed in on the rebels, and a small clash ensued at Bramham Moor, where the Yorkists won a negligible victory. Still, the Earl of Lincoln managed to avoid the main bulk of Henry Tudor's army: the latter suddenly disengaged and moved off after hearing that the city of York was attacked. This was a planned diversion by the rebellious Yorkists, and it succeeded. After this, the Yorkist army crossed the Trent River and set their positions on top of a hill, close to the village of East Stoke. What ensued was the Battle of Stoke Field, fought on July 17th, 1487. Oddly enough, this battle is often "overlooked" as a minor, insignificant confrontation, but it was - by all accounts - a larger and far bloodier battle than Bosworth Field.

Before the battle began, the House of Tudor had 12,000 troops deployed, facing some 8,000 Yorkist rebels. However, the terrain and the battle positions led the armies into close quarter, attritional combat that resulted in heavy casualties and ferocious fighting. It should not be out of place to say that the Yorkist army was at a disadvantage. It had the numerical disadvantage, for starters, and was also ill-equipped compared to the Lancastrians. Furthermore, the leading commanders of Tudor's forces, Jasper Tudor the Earl of Pembroke and John de Vere the Earl of Oxford, were quite seasoned and capable leaders. However, some noted historians state that the Yorkist did have one advantage over the enemy, and that was a *core of well-trained foreign mercenaries*. Either way, the battle soon ensued. The Yorkists under Lincoln were arrayed in a single formation, rooted in the high ground, while the army of Henry Tudor was deployed in three battle formations: vanguard, center, and rearguard. Throughout the battle, only the vanguard - commanded by the Earl of Oxford - was committed. The opening stages of the Battle of Stoke Field were marked by a devastating arrow volley against the Yorkists. Lincoln saw that he had to act, and thus he immediately went on the attack in hopes of swarming and turning the vanguard of the Lancastrian army. He caused great casualties amongst his enemy by doing so but failed to send them on the retreat. The Earl of Oxford rallied his shaken men and managed to hold on. What ensued was a bitter, ferocious attrition fight that lasted for three hours, with casualties mounting on both sides. Alas, the attrition combat meant that Yorkist troops could not endure, being at a numerical disadvantage. This, and the continued barrage of precise arrow fire, decimated their ranks.

Contemporary accounts state that after the battle, some Yorkist corpses were "like hedgehogs", pierced by many arrows. In the end, their army was routed, and fled. Their escape routes were, however, limited, and many were cut down while eloping down a narrow ravine. Most of the leading Yorkist commanders were also killed in the battle. This included John de la Pole, the Earl of Lincoln. Only Francis Lovell, Viscount Lovell, managed to escape with his life, but his fate afterwards remains a mystery to this day, as he was never heard from again. Young Lambert Simnel was captured alive, but Henry VII chose to spare him, realizing that he was a simple boy who was used by Lincoln and the Yorkists. Simnel worked in Tudor's kitchens as a scullion and spit-turner, and in his later life as a falconer.

The Battle of Stoke Field was the last military engagement of the Wars of the Roses. It effectively crushed the Yorkist cause and cemented Henry VII on the throne as the first King of the Tudor Dynasty. The death of John de la Pole - a Plantagenet by ancestry - did not, however, end the Yorkist threat. There was still his younger brother, the Duke of Suffolk - Edmund de la Pole - who was a leading Yorkist claimant to the throne until he was executed by Henry Tudor's successor in 1513. There was also their younger brother, Richard de la Pole, who also continued his claims to the throne until he died in Italy at the Battle of Pavia in 1525. In the end, there only remained William de la Pole, the fourth brother, who was kept as a captive in the Tower of London for 37 years, where he died in 1539.

Oddly enough, the false claim of Lambert Simnel was not the only one during the early years of Henry VII's reign. In 1491, there stepped forward one Perkin Warbeck, a young man who was falsely proclaimed as Richard of Shrewsbury, one of the two child "Princes in the Tower", sons of Edward IV that disappeared during the ascension of Richard III. It is said that he was very similar in appearance to late Edward IV. This new impostor was seen as a favorable Yorkist claimant: in 1490, being present at the Burgundian court, Warbeck proclaimed that he was Richard of Shrewsbury and that he was not killed as a child for being so young. Margaret of York, sister of Edward IV, formally recognized him as Richard IV of England, and the man became recognized as the Duke of York amongst the European nobility. Henry Tudor protested heavily all the while.

Warbeck's claims were pressed for two years, as his many European supporters and patrons benefited from the intrigues and unrest of the English royal court. Both in England, and abroad, Warbeck's (Richard of Shrewsbury) cause gained support from leading Yorkists such as Sir William Stanley, Sir Thomas Thwaites, Sir Simon Montfort, and Sir Robert Clifford, amongst others. However, Henry Tudor's spies managed to infiltrate the core of this conspiracy in the winter of 1494-1495, arresting a large number of the prominent Yorkist conspirators. Amongst them were Lord Fitzwater and Sir William Stanley, the latter being beheaded promptly. Many others were hanged or imprisoned.

Still, this new Yorkist cause was not fully extinguished. Perkin Warbeck sailed from Flanders in July 1495, having amassed an army of some 2,000 exiled Yorkists and many German mercenaries. He landed in England, but his forces were soon destroyed by Kentish levies, and he had to flee to Ireland. There he landed in Munster. However, Henry Tudor anticipated his route and sent his man, Sir Edward Poynings, there to quell Warbeck's supporters. Because of this, Warbeck found only the Earl of Desmond as his supporter in Ireland. In time, however, Warbeck sought to capitalize on the popular uprising that erupted in Cornwall. This rebellion was raised by the Cornish people who were opposing harsh taxes and generally resented Henry VII. The rebel army marched on London, sweeping through five counties along the way before being stopped by a vicious fight at Blackheath. Perkin Warbeck now sought to use their resentment of Henry Tudor. He landed at Devon and gathered a force of 8,000 rebels. He was proclaimed as Richard IV of England at a gathering at Bodmin Moor. The army first marched on Exeter, finding the city closed to him. Warbeck attempted a siege of the city, but soon found out that a royal army was dispatched to lift the siege. He then advanced on Taunton, but there discovered that his troops were so dispirited that a defeat seemed a certainty. He panicked and deserted his army, fleeing to an abbey where he was caught. In exchange for his life, he confessed his fraud and revealed his true identity. Subsequently he was imprisoned in the Tower of London. In 1498 he attempted to escape - without success. This earned him stricter imprisonment in the dungeons. In 1499 he planned another escape, this time aided by the young Edward Plantagenet of Clarence the ex-Earl of Warwick. Again, Henry VII foiled their attempts: the two were caught and soon after executed. This allowed Henry to effectively get rid of a young Plantagenet claimant, Edward of Clarence, without needing to come up with an excuse. Some say that at the time of his death, young Clarence was mentally unstable and feeble, because of the long time he spent imprisoned in the Tower of London and its dungeons. Contemporary accounts state that he was so long kept away *"out of all company of men, and sight of beasts, in so much that he could not discern a goose from a capon."* When he died, the House of Plantagenet was thus effectively extinct in the legitimate male line. And it was with his demise that the Wars of the Roses truly ended. The military engagements surrounding the rising of Perkin Warbeck were the true last engagements of these grueling, lengthy wars.

Chapter VIII

With the last of the pretenders and plotters finally subdued, Henry VII's hold on the throne was now secure. Oddly enough, his reign thus unfolded with plenty of peace and prosperity. He was quite successful in restoring stability and power to England and was described as a tempered and prudent monarch. Unlike most of his Yorkist predecessors, Henry Tudor attained the throne without having any experience in managing an estate or let alone a realm and lacked key experience in financial administration. Even so, he proved himself as a rather capable ruler in all spheres. A number of his policies and taxations served to dispense with outdated practices and to curb the power of the nobility, and thus fill the realm's near-empty coffers. In no time he became a "fiscally prudent monarch", fully restoring the stable financial state of the realm that was near bankruptcy even during Henry VI's reign. He kept the same financial advisors throughout his reign, which further added to the financial stability. Throughout his reign, the two Lords High Treasurer were Baron Dynham and the Earl of Surrey. In previous decades, these positions were frequently changed, which only added to the instability. Of course, in order to improve the realm's finances, Henry VII had to introduce new, bold, and ruthless taxes. In the early years of his reign, these taxes were met with disdain, especially in Cornwall. Nevertheless, they remained, and worked splendidly to fill England's coffers. Notably, Henry created increased taxes for the nobility by judging that if they spent either a lot or little - they could equally pay his new, increased taxes. The policy worked.

Personally, Henry VII was a moderate and composed man. He was noted for not showing much emotion in public, giving off his iconic aura of composure and patience. His marriage to Elizabeth of York was one of loyalty and love - by all accounts. In stark contrast to his predecessors, Henry Tudor was noted as a loyal husband who had no affairs. To that end, many contemporaries stated that the royal marriage of the Tudors was one of mutual affection and stability. The pair had several children, of which their eldest son, Arthur, was the heir apparent to the throne. Alas, misfortune struck Henry VII's later life. On April 2nd, 1502, at age 15, Arthur the Prince of Wales, Henry's heir, suddenly died in the Welsh Marches, at Ludlow Castle. He suffered for a short while from an enigmatic and incurable sickness at the time, known as the English Sweating Sickness. Two days later, the news reached the royal court and King Henry VII. At the time he was asleep, and was awoken by his confessor who spoke quoting Job from the Bible: *"If we receive good things at the hands of God, why may we not endure evil things?"* He then proceeded to tell him that *"his dearest son hath departed to God"*. Henry Tudor received the news with utter shock and great sadness. It is said that he wept and sobbed overcome by grief, which came as a stark contrast to his usually composed and calm nature. The news was then broken to Queen Elizabeth of York, who mourned equally, yet attempted to console her husband by reminding him that they still had *"a fair Prince and two fair princesses and that God is where he was, and they were both young enough."* However, she soon after collapsed in grief, sobbing.

Sadly, that was not the end of misfortune for Henry VII. In 1502, Elizabeth became pregnant again, and on February 2nd, 1503, she gave birth to a daughter. However, the child died just a few days after. Elizabeth grieved and succumbed to postpartum fever, dying on February 11th - her 37th birthday. The news of her death utterly devastated Henry Tudor. Contemporaries state that he was "broken-hearted" and overcome by grief. He shut himself in solitary confinement and would see nobody. In short, he became a mere shadow of himself, worn out by grief. He became ill himself and despondent, and he died of tuberculosis at Richmond Palace on the 21st of April 1509.

Henry VII was succeeded peacefully by his son, who became King Henry VIII. His reign lasted for some 38 years, and was largely successful and influential, albeit a bit controversial. He is best remembered for marrying six times, annulling three of these marriages and executing two wives on grounds of treason. His reign was also marked with his great disagreement with Pope Clement VII about the annulment of his marriage, that Henry decided to boldly initiate the English Reformation, through which he separated from the papal authority and established an independent Church of England - of which he became the Supreme Head. He also - perhaps infamously - initiated the Dissolution of the Monasteries, an act for which the Pope excommunicated him. But nevertheless, Henry VIII was seen as a successful English King, and by many historians as the "most important" ruler in English history and "one of the most charismatic rulers to sit on the English throne". By all means, he was one of the most successful of the Tudor Dynasty monarchs. He introduced radical changes to the English constitution, continuing to oppose papal power and introducing the theory of the divine right of kings. Through all this, royal power was greatly increased in his time. Notoriously, however, Henry VIII did not shy away from charges of treason and regular executions in order to rid himself of opponents and dissenters. Many of his enemies at court were executed without even a formal trial. For this he was often described as a tyrant. Whoever fell out of Henry's favor was going to be undoubtedly exiled or executed. But more than anything, Henry VIII was extremely rich. Through the Dissolution of the Monasteries and the acts of Reformation, he made himself - and the realm - very wealthy. The money that previously went to Rome and to the Pope, he used to fill his royal coffers. Henry VIII was known as an extravagant spender, ever dancing on the thin edge between wealth and bankruptcy. His conflicts and wars with France and Scotland continued to exert a financial toll on England, as did his lavish new projects and continuous personal spending. Either way, historians and contemporaries describe him as an accomplished, capable, decisive, confident, and attractive King and certainly one of the best to lead England. Still, in his later life he gained a reputation for tyranny, egotism, overindulgence, and lustfulness. Around this time, he also became overweight. He died in 1547 and was succeeded by his young son Edward VI.

About King Richard III

But what about that central figure of the Wars of the Roses who was often confined to the sidelines, without a proper spotlight on him. We are talking about the Duke of Gloucester, later King Richard III. Has he been misunderstood by history? Portrayed as a false villain? Many claim that Richard III was misunderstood in history and is a victim of the classic "history written by the victors". Of course, the main source for his negative image in history is his alleged murder of his two nephews, the young sons of Edward IV - the Princes in the Tower. Without a doubt, of course, he would have motives to do this: they were a direct obstacle for his path to kingship. But no one could ever claim with certainty that he did so. Some, in fact, proposed that the boys were killed on orders from Henry Tudor - for whom they would equally be an obstacle to the throne. Subsequent to the Battle of Bosworth Field and Richard's death in battle, much has been said about him that can be seen as slander and deliberate negative portrayal. Was Richard III a great ruler made bad by his enemies? Much pinpoints to the case being such. Many of Richard's contemporaries unbiasedly wrote of him as a "good lord" with a "great heart", who punished "oppressors of the commons". His apparent kindness and good nature were often mentioned by foreign visitors to the court, and he was quick to win them over with his charisma. One of the institutions that he created in his short reign was the Court of Requests, a specially appointed court for the commoners, those who were so poor and could not afford legal representation. Here, their troubles could be heard and resolved. Furthermore, he improved bail, helping to protect suspected felons from unjust imprisonment before their trial, and to protect their property from seizure until they were proven guilty or innocent. Richard III also banned restrictions on the printing and sale of books, and also ordered the translation of the written Laws and Statutes from French into English, so as to make them more available to the English people. He also established the Herald's College or College of Arms in London, a very important institution. Besides all this, he made many more laws and acts that were seen as beneficial to the people. All in all, he was seen as a great promoter of legal fairness.

One thing was often used by his enemies to create a negative image of him: and that is his crooked back. In truth, Richard III suffered from debilitating scoliosis that made one of his shoulders significantly higher than the other. Besides this, he was seemingly of short stature, which meant that he was often described as a "hunchback" and as "ill-deformed". These physical attributes were easily linked to him in portrayal of a villain. Upon the discovery of Richard III's remains in Leicester, the physical deformation was apparent:

"A very pronounced curve in the spine was visible when the body was first uncovered, evidence of scoliosis which may have meant that Richard's right shoulder was noticeably higher than his left....The type of scoliosis seen here is known as idiopathic adolescent onset scoliosis. The word idiopathic means that the reason for its development is not entirely clear, although there is probably a genetic component. The term adolescent onset indicates that the deformity wasn't present at birth, but developed after the age of ten. It is quite possible that the scoliosis was progressive..."

But are we to judge a monarch only because of his physical shortcomings? The Tudor supporters certainly did and used their slander and systematic building of Richard III's negative image to cement their grasp on the throne which they won through conquest. Arguably the most influential work that portrayed Richard III as a "hunchbacked villain" and tyrant was Shakespeare's play, Richard III. After this play, it was almost impossible to advocate for a positive image for the actual, historic Richard. This gave rise to many debates amongst historians who are trying to dig deep and uncover the true nature of King Richard III as a ruler. Michael Hicks, for example, in his noted 1986 book *"Richard III as Duke of Gloucester: a study in character"*, states quite one-sidedly:

"Richard's selfishness denotes both exceptional egotism and individualism. Whereas other magnates thought in the long-term, seeking to maintain the family estates and to foster the interests of future generations of their dynasty, Richard gave priority to his own good, his immediate political needs and the eventual salvation of his soul. He was concerned only secondarily with the long-term interests of his heirs, whom he disinherited by his alienations in mortmain and otherwise. If Richard's career as Duke of Gloucester fails to make sense, it is because his aims were different from those of other magnates. Both as duke and king, Richard appreciated that heirs strengthened his own position by giving permanence to his tenure, but he did not acknowledge any obligation to give priority to their interests over his own. One wonders whether his sentimental attachments to the houses of York and Neville were sincere or were merely further expressions of Richard's self-interest. Certainly, his seizure of the crown sacrificed the interests of his wider kindred to himself and led ultimately to the destruction of the royal house to which they all belonged."

However, one of the best modern writers on the topic of Richard III, Annette Carson, fights to portray Richard III as the last true good guy in the Wars of the Roses, brutally usurped by the covetous Henry Tudor. In her monumental 2009 work, *"Richard III: The Maligned King"*, she poignantly writes:

"In the age of chivalry, and in the very year when Caxton published Malory's Morte d'Arthur with its uplifting theme of knightly virtue and purity, England found itself under the heel of a king whose very first act [stripping and parading Richard's corpse] was one of calculated barbarity. By contrast, Richard III's end would prove to represent England's last personification of the monarch as the flower of chivalry: the last king leading his men shoulder to shoulder in battle, but more than that, attempting to curtail the bloodshed by settling the outcome in single combat."

And only from that single excerpt, we can deduce a lot about Richard III's true nature. Despite his physical shortcomings he was noted as a capable fighter and war leader. With one brave charge - what seemed to be certain death - he decided to put his own life forward in order to decide the fate of the realm. Did Henry Tudor respond in equal measure? Or did he stand back as his knights surrounded Richard and murdered him? A lot still has to be answered, and many details have to be observed from the sidelines, as it is quite easy to speak of individual monarchs of the Wars of the Roses from a biased point of view. Nevertheless, it might be unjust to think of Richard III as a cruel and tyrannical monarch, when - judging by all the evidence - he was a man quite opposite to that. Can the wrongs be righted? And can we start seeing King Richard III in a different light? Perhaps.

Chapter IX

Without a doubt, the Wars of the Roses made a considerable impact on the English society of the time, and in many ways changed the flow of history of that nation. However, the scale of that impact has been largely debated amongst historians over the centuries. It is true that many parts of England were not affected by the wars, and many believe that the Wars of the Roses were somewhat exaggerated in the generations that followed. Nevertheless, they did happen, and they did entail a near-endless number of pretenders and key players. Still, those amongst you with a keen historian's eye will quickly notice that the Wars of the Roses were somewhat unlike the other wars in Europe of the time. There were no grand strategies, no massive armies, and - most of all - no protracted sieges. It was a war of swift decisions, of intrigue and conspiracies, revolts and decisive, pitched battles.

Some historians state that the royals and the nobles involved on both sides in these wars understood that they too had *a lot* to lose by descending into bitter all-out warfare. The destruction of the land that would undoubtedly ensue would benefit no one - especially if we take into account that the monarchs often changed positions. It is likely because of this that the Wars of the Roses were marked with several decisive pitched battles where leaders attempted to resolve the war with a great victory. Without a shred of doubt, it was the nobles of England that paid the heaviest toll in these wars. Many noble houses were entirely extinguished as a consequence, with fathers, sons, and heirs perishing in battles - often in a single day. Most notably, of course, the wars extinguished the male lines of both the Houses of Lancaster and York. Furthermore, the male line of the Beaufort family was extinct, as well as most of the male descendants of the Neville family. As a result of their demise, their influence and wealth was transferred to Henry Tudor, greatly increasing his power. Some sources state that before the war broke out there were some 60 major noble families in England. However, after the wars ended, that number was reduced to 30. This was of course increased because of many personal feuds between individual families, such as the Percy-Neville feud. Several of the nobles were "forced" to enter the conflict because of their dynastic connections, relations, marriage ties, and so on. While a majority of the common soldiers that were a part of a noble's retinue were allowed to live and return to freedom after the war, the knights, nobles, and the rest of the gentry were not as lucky.

The Wars of the Roses were noted for their "no quarter" policy that was seemingly in use in its every part. This meant that captive nobles were no longer held for ransom - as no one was willing to pay it. Of course, there was that simple fact that if such a captive noble was left alive, they would simply get another chance to fight for their cause and prolong the conflict. So it was that many captive nobles were executed without mercy, be they young or old. And this was quick to lead to extinctions in the male line. Such is the nature of dynastic conflicts, where even young boys are seen as a threat simply because of their noble surname and the connection to the throne. A clear example is the death of Edward of Westminster, the son and heir of King Henry VI. The boy, aged 17, was present at the Battle of Tewkesbury, a defeat of his Lancastrian faction. Following the battle, some enemy soldiers found the boy in a grove, weeping. The boy pleaded for his life but was nonetheless cruelly beheaded, simply because he was an heir of the Lancastrian cause. Many such examples exist in the Wars of the Roses and show us that this was a war of the nobility, a true dynastic war where the rich and the powerful descended into an all-out conflict that was to determine who was the true "king of the jungle." And all that at the expense of the common men and women.

The Wars of the Roses claimed around 105,000 lives in total, which is a comparatively low number considering that the wars lasted some 32 years in total. Nevertheless, this number equaled to 5.5% of the entire English population in 1450, which is a percentage that cannot be disregarded. The matters were undoubtedly made worse by the spread of the Black Death, or the Bubonic Plague, which swept through England almost exactly one hundred years before the onset of the Wars of the Roses. The plague decimated England's citizens and caused the death of up to 60% of its entire population. After this initial outbreak, the Black Death kept returning at intervals, always claiming more lives. It occurred even during the Wars of the Roses. In the decades between 1430 and 1480, it returned quite strongly, with a serious outbreak in 1471 that claimed some 15% of the entire population. Another outbreak around 1480 claimed 20%. All of this tells us that England's population at the time was quite low, and that 105,000 casualties of the Wars of the Roses are not a small number after all. Even with the end of the wars and the Tudor Dynasty now firmly on the throne of England, the shadow of the Yorkist claims still existed, although remote. Some called this "paranoia" and senseless fear, but in fact, it was not quite so senseless after all. A serious *military* threat was, of course, not present, but there was that prospect that the Wars of the Roses could - at some point - erupt all anew. Henry Tudor had to make sure that they would not. The main threat were the individuals that could trace their descent from the Plantagenet family and could thus challenge the Tudor claim and re-ignite the conflict.

At the time of Henry VII's ascendance to the throne, there were some 18 Plantagenet descendants alive. This number increased greatly by 1510, as 16 Yorkist children were born in the meantime. The chief of these Plantagenet descendants were the members of the De La Pole family. As we mentioned, John de la Pole, the Earl of Lincoln was one of these claimants, but he fell in the Battle of Stoke Field. His brother, the Duke of Suffolk, openly pressed his claim to the throne and Henry VII had him executed because of it in 1513. That still left Richard de la Pole, known as the "White Rose," as the last serious Yorkist pretender to the English crown. After his brothers and many relatives were executed by the Tudors, Richard lived in exile in Europe, where he openly conspired to assemble an army and invade England in order to reclaim the throne. He was a maternal descendant of Richard the Duke of York. In Europe, he enjoyed the support of several rulers and nobles who saw interest in the continuation of distress in England.

By 1514, Richard the White Rose amassed an army of 12,000 German mercenaries, and attempted to sail over to England, but nothing came of this. Afterwards, he established himself in the court of the French King Francis I, where he was given support in 1523 to invade England together with the Scottish regent, John Stewart the Duke of Albany. The invasion was not carried out immediately, however. Richard was then present alongside King Francis I at the Battle of Pavia in 1525. The battle was a major defeat for the French, and Richard de la Pole the White Rose, the Duke of Suffolk, was killed in the fighting while commanding the infantry. His death was seen as a major relief by the Tudors, who now had one less major Yorkist claimant to deal with. The other Plantagenet descendants continued to be a known threat for the Tudors but were not so open with their claims to the throne.

As late as 1600, there existed 12 competitors for the succession of the throne, and seven of those were Plantagenet descendants. The Tudors knew that they had a tenuous claim to the throne, and that is why a considerable part of Henry VIII's reign was marked with increased anxiety over his producing a male heir to the throne. His first son, Henry the Duke of Cornwall, died within weeks of his birth, and it wasn't until 1537 that his son Edward VI was born. A competent monarch, Henry VIII knew all too well that the risk of a succession crisis was great, and that instilled fear of the renewed Wars of the Roses. Nevertheless, by his time there was a much greater stability in the realm and that lessened the chances of a new conflict arising. Much of that stability is credited to Henry VII, whose capable leadership gave England the prosperity it needed. When he ascended to the throne, the governmental structure was nearly in shambles. He then managed to deal with early uprisings and threats, and to address all the important parts of the realm with functionality, determination, and shrewdness that were all the aspects of a capable and confident monarch. In no time, trade, commerce, culture, arts, and literature all flourished. There would be no civil war in England in the next 155 years.

"Henry's (Henry VII) genius was mainly a genius for cautious maneuver, for exact timing, for delicate negotiation, for weighing up an opponent or a subordinate, and not least, a genius for organization. He was a competent soldier, but always chose peace instead of war as being so much cheaper and so much safer." "The mask he wore was to some extent deliberately inhuman. He wished to be remote and incalculable; he wished to be more feared than loved."

Of course, this meant that by the time Henry VIII came to the throne, he inherited from his father a stable economy and a prosperous England, upon which he only built further, despite his lavish lifestyle and great spending. He strengthened the authority of the monarchy, thanks to his concept of the "divine rights of kings" and brought a new independence for the Church of England and increased wealth by the dissolution of monasteries. All the good policies of his father allowed Henry VIII to be a successful and well-liked king, who did not fail in the role of a monarch. The noted British historian from the University of Warwick, John Joseph Scarisbrick, paints a praiseful picture of Henry VIII:

"He had survived pretenders, excommunication, rebellion and threats of invasion, died in his bed and passed his throne peacefully to his heir. He had won a title, Defender of the Faith, which English monarchs still boast... He had made war on England's ancient enemies and himself led two assaults on France. For nearly four decades he had cut an imposing figure in Europe...bestriding its high diplomacy as few of his predecessors, if any, had done. He had defied the pope and the emperor, brought into being in England and Ireland a national Church subject to his authority, wiped about a thousand religious houses off the face of his native

land...and bestowed on English kingship a profound new dignity. He...had brought the Scriptures in the vernacular to his people, hesitantly and perhaps partly unwittingly, but nonetheless decisively, allowed his country to be directed towards the continental Reformation...and given to his people a new sense of unity – the unity of 'entire Englishmen' rather than that of 'Englishmen papisticate' or of those who were 'scarce our subjects'. The England which he had led back into European affairs...had disowned allegiance to any external authority, indisputably emerged from his reign with a new political 'wholeness'... [...] His reign had given England much 'good governance'."

At this point we have to ask the question; would it be the same under the Yorkists? What fate would befall England if King Richard III was victorious at Bosworth Field, and remained at England's helm? What would have happened if the Stanley brothers chose to assist Richard? Although his reign was short, it showed immense potential, especially for the common folk. Would his attention to the common citizen earn him the enmity of the nobles? Or would he and his successors be plagued by Lancastrian pretenders? Would England break away from papal authority as it did under the Tudors? We will never know for sure what a Yorkist England would look like. The fates had an altogether different plan. After all, if the Wars of the Roses had a different outcome than they did, England as we know it today might not exist at all. We cannot disregard the fact that England entered into a new era under the rule of the Tudors. The Wars of the Roses marked a distinct shift from the Medieval period in England and into the infancy of the English Renaissance. The prominent British historian, John Guy, argues that *"England was economically healthier, more expansive, and more optimistic under the Tudors than at any time since the Roman occupation."* And there is truth in that claim, certainly. Many historians consider the reign of Henry VIII's daughter, Elizabeth I, as a golden age of English history, a period known as the Elizabethan Era, where British pride and culture reached all new heights. It was a time where

English literature, poetry, art, and music flourished, as did architecture, commerce, and naval exploration. It was the age of Shakespeare, of plays and theater, of Sir Francis Drake and his naval exploration. All of these achievements would not be possible without a good monarch that was Queen Elizabeth I, and her father, Henry VIII. For after all, the Tudor rulers laid down a foundation of stability that was continually built upon in order to finally reach the golden age in England. Richard Bucholz and Newton Key, in their influential 2009 book *"Early Modern England, 1485-1714: A Narrative History"*, perfectly tell us how an educated and capable leader such as Elizabeth could have contributed to this bountiful era in English history:

"Like her father, Henry VIII, with whom she identified publicly, she was a larger-than-life personality. This much is inarguable. Elizabeth was young when she took the throne: 25 years old. She was also good-looking - an advantage that she was not reluctant to exploit. In addition, the new queen was highly intelligent, witty, hardworking, and well educated. She was fluent in Latin, French, Spanish, Italian, and, of course, English. She wrote poetry and could speak effectively when she chose to do so. Elizabeth was also, like her father, something of a scholar: she once translated Boethius' "On the Consolations of Philosophy" into English for her own amusement. She also took after her father in being both musical and athletic. She played the virginals (a primitive keyboard instrument), danced, and hunted with enthusiasm. A final, crucial similarity to Henry VIII was that Elizabeth I was vain and imperious. Men could flirt with her - indeed, she encouraged them - but they had to be careful not to go too far, for she never forgot that she was queen."

Chapter X

Of course, when writing about the Wars of the Roses, we have to consider the military aspect, the weapons and the tactics of the time. Arguably, these wars were not as complex in a military sense as some others of the time, but they still involved heavy battles of the classic medieval style. One major difference, however, was the lack of sieges, which were a major aspect of warfare in the medieval period. England had an abundance of castles and fortresses at the time, but the vast majority of the battles in the Wars of the Roses were waged outside of them. The main use for the castles was as shelters for the innocent populace, especially when large armies were on the march. For example, the Lancastrians, early in the Wars of the Roses, had a nasty reputation for pillaging. Yorkist castles acted as a safe haven for the distraught commoners. To that end, most of this dynastic conflict was resolved in the open field, in the classic pitched line battles that were becoming somewhat of a rarity. Of this we wrote above: these battles were seen as a clear opportunity for the leading kings and pretenders to be killed and their armies routed and crushed, thus ending the wars quickly. Alas, in the Wars of the Roses there was always a new claimant to the throne, ready to replace a fallen one. The nobles were the main cause for the non-destructive character of the Wars of the Roses, as it were them who sought out pitched battles in the first place.

Another aspect in which the Wars of the Roses diverged from the norm is the lack of that iconic medieval chivalry. We can imagine the middle ages as an era of knights and nobles, splendid and elegant, enhanced by their chivalric traditions of mercy, honor, and respect. In the Wars of the Roses, however, all of this became null and void. Of course, the practice was in decline well before the Wars erupted. This meant that the aged practices of mutual respect and honor between enemy nobles were no longer viable. Once, a noble would go to great lengths just to spare his enemy, to capture them alive and ransom them for money. In the 1400's, this was not efficient, as this only allowed for a future continuation of the conflict, with everything potentially going in circles.

At the time of the Hundred Years' War and the Battle of Crecy (August 26th, 1346), almost a century before the Wars of the Roses, it was obvious that chivalry was dead. Here, English longbowmen devastated the heavily armed French nobles without mercy. The bulk of French nobility was left dead on the battlefield, cut down viciously, with many noble houses going extinct in a single day. No ransoms, no mercy, no captivity: just death. So, it should not come as a surprise to know that by the mid-1400s, chivalry was becoming outdated. With the dynastic nature of these wars, it was clear that killing an enemy noble gained so much more than keeping them alive. Contemporary accounts tell us this directly: Edward IV was noted for ordering his troops to kill all the nobles, and spare captive commoners. With leading nobles dead, and entire noble houses extinct, the opposing side would inevitably lose in the war. At the Battle of Barnet, the Neville's were near-extinguished, while after the Battle of Towton some 42 captured knights and nobles were mercilessly executed. It was a cruel war, no doubt, where greed, the lust for power and that coveted throne of England reigned over any idea of chivalry.

As far as the weaponry and tactics go, the Wars of the Roses placed an emphasis on infantry, and the efficient use of flanking attacks. In most of the major battles that were fought, you can notice the pattern of simple line formations: three "battles" (divisions) facing the opposing three directly. These were the battles of attrition and decisive strikes, where a quick folding of a flank could end the battle swiftly. The English gentry usually fought on foot rather than in the saddle. They were, however, heavily armored and armed, with their suits of armor and helmets, and many were hampered by this, especially when facing longbowmen or getting stuck in marshy ground. In this period, a full suit of medieval knight's armor weighed no more than 15kg (33lbs).

In fact, many say that the likes of the Earl of Warwick the Kingmaker, and of King Richard III, died while fighting on foot. Undoubtedly, it was far more expensive to field heavily armored knightly cavalry than simple infantry, and that led to the shift in their use in the Wars of the Roses. To that end, the battles saw increased use of longbowmen, who were a devastating and potent weapon when used properly. A series of heavy arrow barrages could turn the tide of the battle, and English leaders knew it all too well. Subsequently, many new tactics were developed in order to counter the advantage of longbowmen, such as closing gaps quickly, developing new knightly armor, or increasing the space between opposing armies.

One of the novelties that began appearing on battlefields around this time is artillery. Many primitive guns and cannons existed, and their efficiency in battles was arguable. These were the iconic arquebuses and primitive hand cannons, and they were used in extremely limited numbers. There also existed the so-called "Organ Guns," or ribauldequins, guns with multiple barrels that yielded a much higher rate of fire. However, the rise of the classic bombard rendered many of the primitive cannons obsolete almost overnight. Powerful large caliber artillery, the bombard was effective in sieges. In 1464, Bamburgh Castle was captured by the Kingmaker after a nine-month siege, thanks to these bombards.

However, in the end, it all came down to the bitter fighting on the ground. The infantryman, the knight, the bowman. It was they who decided the fates of the realm, fighting in the mud and the blood for the nobles they supported. In fact, most of the battles of the Wars of the Roses were just that: classic attrition battles where two armies "duked it out". But these were the battles where chivalry took its last dying breaths, where gallant knights were a rarity, and where personal interests always came out on top. It was an age of bitterness and great malice, where the crown was attained quickly - but lost equally fast.

Conclusion

Without a doubt, the Wars of the Roses gave great inspiration to authors and artists over the centuries. Its events were the subject of many great paintings and art pieces created in subsequent years, and it became a great milestone in overall English history. Undoubtedly, the most famous author to have written on the subject of these wars was William Shakespeare. Shakespeare was born in 1564 and died in 1616. This tells us that he wrote over a century following the end of the Wars of the Roses. Interestingly, they were not called that in his time since that name arose in the 19th century. In the late 1500's they were called simply the "civil wars." Either way, Shakespeare took great inspiration in this conflict, and was one of the earliest authors to offer a fictionalized account of them. This resulted in his most popular and renowned plays: Henry VI, Richard III, Richard II, Henry IV, Henry V, and so on. The works of Shakespeare are considered as the most iconic ever written in the English language, and these plays only served to bring the subject of the Wars of the Roses closer to the general public. However, many of these plays can be seen as biased and written from an "anti-Yorkist" perspective and served to give further validity to the Tudor claim.

A more modern "classic" that was undoubtedly inspired by the complexity of the Wars of the Roses is the famed "A Song of Ice and Fire" series of novels written by George R. R. Martin, of which "A Game of Thrones" is the most popular title. These novels follow a series of fictional dynasties and noble families, all vying for the throne of the "Seven Kingdoms," set on an island much akin to Britain. In the books there are a lot of colorful characters, some evil, some good, all ultimately fighting for the interests of their respective noble families. When comparing closely the Wars of the Roses and the "Game of Thrones," one can clearly spot the similarities and the inspiration that the author found in real historic events. Bastard sons, heraldry, heirs presumptive, mad kings and king-slayers, powerful noble families and poor upstarts, ill-advisers, endless battles, and above all - tons of intrigue. These are the defining features of both the historic Wars of the Roses, and the popular fantasy novels by Martin. So, if you loved the Lannisters and the Baratheons, the Targaryens and the Starks, you should know that they had much the same historic counterparts, and that only makes all of it that much more interesting.

Of course, there exist many contemporary accounts of the Wars of the Roses, for which historians can be quite thankful. These conflicts arose in a time when literacy was on the rise and historiography was in its foundations. Thus, we have several key contemporary chronicles of the wars, such as Warkworth's Chronicle written around 1500, the Croyland Chronicle (1449–1486), the crucial writings of Philippe de Commines, Capgrave's Chronicle (1464), and the writings of Jean de Waurin. All of these allowed historians to present the story of the Wars of the Roses in great detail, a fact from which we can all benefit today. In the end, there is a lot that we can learn from the Wars of the Roses, both on a greater scale, and on a personal, deeper level. For above all, these wars are a story. A story of injustice, of wronged individuals, and of personal greed. Of blemished ideals and high-soarers, of cruel opportunists and unyielding war-leaders. It is a mix of man's best and worst attributes, combined into one deadly mixture that decided on the fates of men. Of kingmakers - and king-undoers.

Using the same line with which we opened this book, we can also close it: *about empty thrones a lot can be said.* A vacant throne is a deadly thing: it lures in and leads either to death or short-lived glory. Many were blinded by its glare and never attained it. From Henry VI to Edward IV, and then on to Richard III and Henry VII - many have tried to gain it, but most were not seated upon it long enough. It was a hard to gain reward, slippery from all the blood that established it in the first place. Such is the tale of thrones. In the end, the Wars of the Roses displayed all those chief aspects of the medieval gentry: greed, pride, ambition, and stubborn perseverance. And for their vain ideals, the common man bled: that foot soldier who was neither a Yorkist nor a Lancastrian, but rather a commoner who was in the wrong place at the wrong time. It is the blood of these commoners that soaks the fields of Britannia, and that has won many a crown for would-be kings.

References:

Carpenter, C. 1997. *The Wars of the Roses: Politics and the Constitution in England, C.1437-1509.* Cambridge University Press.

Cheetham, A. 2000. *The Wars of the Roses.* University of California Press.

Cook, D. R. 2014. *Lancastrians and Yorkists: The Wars of the Roses.* Routledge.

Dockray, K. 2017. *Henry VI, Margaret of Anjou and the Wars of the Roses: From Contemporary Chronicles, Letters and Records.* Fonthill Media.

Dougherty, M. J. 2015. *The Wars of the Roses: The conflict that inspired Game of Thrones.* Amber Books Ltd.

Edgar, J. G. 2020. *The Wars of the Roses.* Books on Demand.

Gillingham, J. 1981. *The Wars of the Roses : Peace and Conflict in Fifteenth-century England.* Louisiana State University Press.

Goodman, A. 1990. *The Wars of the Roses: Military Activity and English Society, 1452-97.* Taylor & Francis.

Gravett, C. 2003. *Towton 1461: England's Bloodiest Battle.* Osprey Publishing.

Gravett, C. 2003. *Tewkesbury 1471: The Last Yorkist Victory.* Osprey Publishing.

Haigh, P. 2001. *From Wakefield to Towton: The Wars of the Roses.* Pen and Sword.

Hill-Ashdown, J. 2015. *The Wars of the Roses.* Amberley Publishing Limited.

Komar, M. 2016. *Engleska u vrijeme Ratova ruža.* J. J. Strossmayer University of Osijek.

Lewis, M. 2015. *The Wars of the Roses: The Key Players in the Struggle for Supremacy.* Amberley Publishing Limited.

Lutkin, J. 2016. *A/AS Level History for AQA The Wars of the Roses, 1450–1499 Student Book.* Cambridge University Press.

Pendrill, C. 2004. *The Wars of the Roses and Henry VII: Turbulence, Tyranny and Tradition in England 1459-c.1513*. Heinemann.

Pollard, A. J. 2013. *The Wars of the Roses*. Macmillan International Higher Education.

Ross, C. 1976. *The Wars of the Roses: A Concise History*. Utopia.

Wagner, J. A. and Wagner, E. E. 2001. *Encyclopedia of the Wars of the Roses*. ABC-CLIO.

Webster, B. 2003. *The Wars of the Roses*. Routledge.

Wise, T. and Embleton, G. A. 1983. *The Wars of the Roses*. Osprey Publishing.

Žgaljardić, K. 2018. *Engleska u Razvijenom Srednjem Vijeku*. University of Pula.

Don't miss out!

Visit the website below and you can sign up to receive emails whenever History Nerds publishes a new book. There's no charge and no obligation.

https://books2read.com/r/B-A-ODOK-EBDYB

BOOKS 2 READ

Connecting independent readers to independent writers.

Also by History Nerds

Celtic History
Ireland

Great Wars of the World
World War 1
World War 2
The Napoleonic Wars: One Shot at Glory
The Serbian Revolution: 1804-1835
Peace Won by the Saber: The Crimean War, 1853-1856
The Wars of the Roses

Irish Heroes
Grace O'Malley: The Pirate Queen of Ireland
William Butler Yeats: Nobel Prize Winning Poet
Scáthach
Finn McCool

The History of the Vikings

Vikings
Longships on Restless Seas

The Rise and Fall of Empires
Rome: The Rise and Fall

Standalone
The History of the United Kingdom
The History of Ireland
The History of America
Stalin
The Fiery Maelstrom of Freedom
The History of Scotland
Robert the Bruce
William Wallace: Scotland's Great Freedom Fighter
The History of Wales

www.ingramcontent.com/pod-product-compliance
Lightning Source LLC
Chambersburg PA
CBHW021018160726
47994CB00006B/2556